Mastering Macarons
Classic to Contemporary Techniques

Colette Christian CMB, CEPC, CEC

ISBN: 978-0-9991071-0-2

Table of Contents

Introduction

This book is designed to be a definitive macaron resource. The go-to-guide to macarons that will save you, the baker, hours of precious time and energy.

What energy? All the energy that is wasted looking for macaron advice reading blogs and watching YouTube videos. The same energy that would be better spent baking batch after batch of beautiful macarons.

Not every source is credible. Are they a real working chef or pastry chef? Where did they study, and who did they work for? Are they certified? Or are they just well-meaning? It is so important to consider your sources.

Macarons have been my Holy Grail for a dozen years. Since my early days as a Le Cordon Bleu Instructor. At that time during a revamping of the school's Pâtisserie and Baking program, it was decided that macarons would be added to PBK121. This was the petit-four module, and one I loved to teach.

The recipe we were given was one from the London Cordon Bleu, and it didn't work well. It is always a challenge when working with recipes that are designed in other places with slight differences in the ingredients.

I was the "fixer" on the pastry faculty and my boss charged me with "fixing" the macaron recipe.

Well, it took some time but eventually the old recipe was replaced with the recipe that is in this book for French macarons. Everyone was much happier, and "macaron" day was no longer dreaded but enjoyed.

This book is written for both professional and home baker.

There are five mixing methods in this book. One is not better than the other, although I do feel that the French technique is the easiest to master. In my teaching class both on ground and online this has always been the case. So this is a great place to start your macaron adventure.

One technique builds on the other, and I hope baking through the book will provide hours of baking satisfaction and beautiful macarons.

☺ ChefColette

Macarons – History and Overview

Like many French pastries – macarons are Italian in origin.

Early macarons were similar in texture to Italian amaretti cookies. These were simply made with sugar, egg whites and almonds. They had a crisp crust and a soft interior, but were more rustic in appearance. The almonds being less finely ground, the egg white was whipped by hand, and the sugar was coarse as well.

The history is vague but there is some research that suggests that they were first made in an Italian monastery, probably one with a few almond trees on the grounds and a little sugar being traded for salvation…

The name of the cookie comes from the Italian word for paste, *maccarone*. The word *maccarone* is derived from the Italian *ammaccare* which means to crush or beat—this refers to the almond meal or paste which is one of the principal ingredients in macarons. The French word *macaronner* means to fold the ingredients for macarons together. This is also known as *macaronnage*, there will be more on this in the techniques chapter.

Recipes for early macarons were brought to France by the pastry cooks with Catherine de Medicis, when she came to France to marry Henri II.

During the French Revolution, two Benedictine nuns, Sister Marguerite and Sister Marie Elisabeth sought asylum in the town of Nancy. The sisters paid for their room and board by making and selling "macaron" cookies. The sisters' recipe was only passed down to family and remained a closely guarded secret for a few hundred years. Recipes for Nancy macarons were not printed until the turn of the 20th century.

In the Nancy macaron, the ratio of powdered sugar to almond meal is 1:1, with an Italian meringue added to it. This recipe is very close to many modern day recipes for macarons.

It wasn't until the 1930s that the hyper elegant macaron of today began to take shape at Ladurée in Paris. Ladurée opened in 1862. Shortly after Madame Ladurée opened up a *salon du thé* (tea room) next to the bakery. It was one of the first public places in Paris, where a woman could sit alone and not appear "loose". It was noted Parisian pastry chef, Pierre Desfontaines Ladurée, who had the brilliant idea of putting ganache between two layers of macarons. These were the first filled macarons.

Chef Pierre's macarons had a finer texture and were lighter. Today, the Ladurée bakeries sells thousands of macarons every week. The Parisian shops sell about 4 million a year. There are Ladurée pastry shops in many international cities. If you are truly macaron obsessed, then a trip to Ladurée is a necessary pilgrimage. If you have already been, then you are agreeing with me.

Ladurée façade in Milan, Italy

Macaron Anatomy and Vocabulary

Shell

Filling

Foot

Shell or Skin:
> The flat top of the macaron. It should be smooth, thin but not overly fragile.

Pied or Foot:
> This is the frilly base of the macaron that we are all obsessed with.
>
> As the moisture from the meringue evaporates and converts into steam— the shell lifts off the surface of the baking sheet. This is how the foot is formed.
>
> There are other factors as well. Proper _pied_ also depends on proper macaronnage, oven temperature, rapping the tray before baking, and letting the macarons form a slight skin before baking.
>
> The foot does not appear until the macarons have been baking for about 8 minutes. This is the point at which I turn on the oven light and check.
>
> Even after all these years, a beautiful lifted "foot" is a wonderful sight to behold.

Macaronnage (from the verb _macaronner_):
> This is the technique of folding the dry ingredients and the meringue together and then removing the excess air from the batter.

Particulates:
> Dry flavorings that can be pulverized with the almonds and powdered sugar. They must be completely dried out. Fruit and vegetable powders, coffee, tea, spices, herbs and cocoa are good flavor enhancers. Remember anything added to the macaron shell must be dry – <u>bone dry</u> – no moisture at all. Watch over-powering flavorings – often a hint of flavor is enough.

Necessary Equipment

Digital Scale that weighs ounces and grams
Macarons demand precision. For successful macaron baking a good scale is an essential piece of equipment.

Stand or Hand Held Mixer
It is much easier to make the meringue in a mixer. A stand mixer with a whisk attachment makes the job easy, but a hand held mixer will also work fine.

Medium Sized Bowl
This is for folding in your dry ingredients (*macaronner* part one) and for knocking out the excess air (*macaronner* part two). It can be any material; metal, glass, ceramic or plastic. The most important thing is that it is wide and big enough to hold the batter, in other words, sufficient surface area. It is impossible to fold if the bowl is too tall or narrow.

Large Flat Spatula
A nice flat spatula is a must. One with a good sturdy handle and a nice flat head. Not a hybrid spatula or one designed to get the mayonnaise out of the jar.

20" Piping Bags
It is easier to pipe your macarons with a longer piping bag, the smaller 12" bags are great for cake decorating but not good for macarons. Reusable or disposable, it's up to you.

Plain Round Tip 3/8" in diameter
Wilton #12 – Ateco #803
This is the recommended size for smaller macarons.

Plain Round Tip
Wilton 1A or Ateco 806
For larger macarons. Any macaron piped larger than 4" in diameter.

Food Processor, large or small
A 4-cup capacity is recommended. But the dry ingredients can be ground ("jushed") in batches.

Candy Thermometer
A digital candy thermometer works best. An instant read thermometer can also be used.

3-4 Heavy Baking Sheets (13"x18")
Macarons do not bake evenly on flimsy sheet pans. The baking sheets should be restaurant grade. They are widely available in cookware stores and restaurant supply stores. Chicago Metallic and Nordic Ware are good brands.

Parchment Paper or Silpats
Both parchment paper and Silpats will work and a paper macaron template can be seen underneath both.

If I have a choice I prefer to bake my macarons on a Silpat—it seems that the foot or *pied* forms slightly better. Recently, "macaron" Silpats have become available. These have circles printed on the silpats. These work well.

I am not a fan of the silicone macaron mats with the raised lip. These can push the foot out and cause it to look more like a "frill" then a foot.

Please do not think that you have to run out and buy Silpats to make pretty macarons. I have piped thousands of macarons onto parchment paper with great results.

Ingredients

A simple almond macaron has four ingredients: blanched almond meal, egg whites, granulated sugar and confectioner's sugar.

Almond Meal

Blanched almond meal is nothing but almonds – skins removed, dried out, and mechanically pulverized. Almond meal is also called almond flour. This is very misleading as there is no wheat or any type of flour added to it. The only ingredient in almond meal is almonds.

The best way to buy almond meal is in bulk. It should be stored it in your freezer. It will keep for 4-5 months in an airtight container. It can be used directly from the freezer.

All nuts and nut meals should be stored in the freezer because of their high oil content. Freezing slows down the process of oxidative rancidity. Oxidative rancidity is the process by which fatty acids break down and lead to rancid off flavors.

Almonds are the driest of all the nuts. That is why they are ideal for macarons.

When macarons are made with other nuts, such as pistachio and hazelnut - almonds are often used as the base nut. When nuts are excessively oily, the oil can separate from the nuts during the baking process and appear on the surface of the shell. Using part almond meal, in conjunction, with nuts that are higher in oil content help absorb some of this excess oil.

Learn more about blending other nuts for macarons on page 56.

Egg Whites

The best egg whites for macarons are "fresh"–separated from whole eggs. Commercial egg white products are not recommended. Often thickeners and whipping agents are added to commercial egg white product. These are guar gum for thickening and triethyl citrate for whipping. Even a small amount of these chemicals can throw off the macaron shell and cause problems.

Egg whites are 90% water and 10% protein. They are naturally alkaline – this reduces the potential for bacterial growth which means egg whites keep well.

They can be stored in the refrigerator in an airtight container for five days. Egg whites will keep in the freezer for up to 4 months.

To thaw frozen egg whites, remove them from the freezer and let them thaw overnight in the refrigerator. This is the safest way to thaw them. The larger the container of egg whites, the longer they will take to thaw.

I thaw mine in 4 ounce containers. That way I am only thawing a small batch at a time. Once egg whites are thawed, it is not advisable to refreeze them. Store thawed leftovers in the refrigerator or make another batch of macarons…

Egg White Powder (also known as Meringue powder)

Egg white powder is dehydrated or dried albumin. It will last indefinitely if kept dry and airtight.

A small amount is used to stabilize meringues. For macarons, this is useful when we use Italian meringue. We add a small amount to the egg whites before we start whipping them.

Egg white powder can also be reconstituted and whipped up into a meringue. It is also food safe as the threat of salmonella is removed in the pasteurization process. The ratio to hydrate egg white powder is 2 tsp of egg white powder to 2 tbsp warm water.

Granulated Sugar

Use pure cane sugar – period. Pure cane sugar (in all its refined glory) is perfect for all types of macarons. Make sure it is labeled 100% pure cane sugar. Premium brands, such as C&H or Domino are recommended.

Lesser store brands may be a mix of cane and beet sugar. Mixing cane and beet sugar lowers the price considerably, so beware if you see a store brand being sold for a great price.

While there is nothing wrong (in general) with beet sugar, it has natural impurities and they can be a problem. These impurities can cause beet sugar to crystallize easily – this is problematic when cooking sugar for syrups and any sort of decorative work.

I don't recommend using organic or superfine sugar. Organic sugar does not have the right texture – it always feels coarser to me than regular sugar, and in testing, macarons made with it were less successful then those made with regular sugar. Superfine sugar is overpriced and not necessary for any of the meringues we make for macarons.

Powdered Sugar
(also known as Confectioner's Sugar, 10X sugar, or Icing Sugar)

Powdered sugar is sucrose crystals (sugar) that have been milled into a fine powder. The number and the X determines the fineness of the sugar.

Cornstarch is also added to powdered sugar to prevent caking. The industry standard is 3% by volume, but in the United States, the amount of cornstarch added to powdered sugar is not regulated by the Food and Drug Administration. So if you see bags of powdered sugar for considerably less than a premium brand it is best to avoid it. It probably has far more cornstarch added to it than 3%.

C&H and Domino follow the industry standard of 3% by volume.

A small amount of cornstarch actually strengthens the shell, but too much cornstarch can cause problems like over dryness and cracking.

It is not necessary to purchase organic powdered sugar for your macarons. It costs 2-3 times the amount of regular powdered sugar and is an unnecessary expense. (When you need to spend up on ingredients, I will let you know.)

Cream of Tartar

Cream of tartar is a bakeshop acid that is used to stabilize egg whites by increasing their heat tolerance and volume retention. This means that when cream of tartar is added in the early stages of making your meringue, it will keep the meringue from collapsing. The ratio of cream of tartar to egg whites is 1/8 tsp (aka a 2 finger pinch) to 4 ounces of egg whites.

Cream of tartar is a byproduct of winemaking and has been used for hundreds of years. It is made from the sediment that was left in the wine barrels. It occurs naturally in grapes, and is the principle acid in winemaking.

It has been used in baking for quite a while now to stabilize egg whites and whipped cream and to make baking powder. The recipe for homemade baking powder is one part baking soda to two parts cream of tartar. Cream of tartar has a shelf life of five years and should be stored in a cool dry place.

SCIENCE SIDEBAR:
Cream of Tartar

Cream of tartar is also known as potassium hydrogen tartrate or potassium bitartrate. It is the potassium salt of tartaric acid.

When we whip egg whites, there are sulfur atoms attached to the edge of the albumin protein molecules.

These sulfur atoms may have a hydrogen atom attached to them. Sometimes these hydrogen atoms release early; they can attach to something else – either another sulfur atom or a protein molecule.

If too many sulfur bonds occur, the proteins pull together too strongly – and the foam collapses.

Because cream of tartar is acidic, the cream of tartar increases the free hydrogen atoms in the liquid. These extra hydrogen atoms keep the sulfur atoms in check. If the sulfur bonds are slowed down then the egg whites will stay stiff long enough to be used.

Essential Tips & Hints for Success

Food color – how to achieve colorful results

Gel colors work for all type of macaron techniques. Gel colors are made with food grade pigment, glycerin and water.

Choosing one with the least water activity is best. This introduces the least amount of extra water into your macaron batter. Supermarket brands are almost all water and should be avoided. Wilton® gel color has the least amount of water activity.

Water soluble powdered color works well with techniques that use a hot sugar syrup. Powdered color is added to the sugar syrup before it is poured on the egg whites. It is possible to achieve strong colors with powdered colors.

One batch... multiple colors

If you want to do multiple colors within one batch, I recommend adding the color when folding in the dry ingredients.

Weigh the processed almond meal and powdered sugar in grams (easiest to divide), divide by the desired number of colors, and set aside.

Then make your meringue adding no color. Weigh the meringue and divide to match your dry ingredients.

Add the color to the meringue and add your dry ingredients in three increments. By the time the dry ingredients are incorporated the color should be mixed evenly.

Flavoring with particulates

Dry flavorings that can be pulverized with the almond and powdered sugar–they must be completely dried out like herbs, teas, and dehydrated fruits. Watch overpowering flavorings–often a hint of the flavor is enough.

Hibernate your macarons for optimal flavor & texture

Macarons are not best fresh. You will find if you bite into one shortly after it comes out of the oven, the outside will be crisp and the inside less tender than purchased in shops.

That's because the macaron needs to "hibernate" or rest in the refrigerator in an airtight container, at least overnight. This is so the sugar in the shell can attract enough (but not too much) moisture and soften the insides. Ideally, when you bite into the macaron the shell is crisp and the inside is soft.

After about 3 days in the refrigerator they can become too soft. Leftover macarons should be stored in the refrigerator in an airtight container. They can also be frozen up to one month.

When thawing macarons, keep the container sealed. If opened the macarons may condensate. It takes 1-2 hours for the macarons to thaw completely.

Macaron production, storage & planning ahead

Once you start making macarons for family, friends and colleagues, you will get many requests. Which is great because you will get a lot of practice. But here are a few tips to get ahead so that you do not have to stay up late baking macarons:

- Shells freeze up to one month. Layer the cooled shells in an airtight container with a sheet of parchment in between each layer.
- Thaw with the container sealed, 1-2 hours.
- Fill the shells 1-2 days before and refrigerate in an airtight container until ready to package or serve.
- Macarons filled with ganache or buttercream may be frozen up to two weeks.

Techniques

Welcome to the Techniques chapter! Here are the five different methods for mixing macarons, covered in detail.

The three classic methods are French, Swiss and Italian. The modern techniques are the Contemporary and my Hybrid Italian.

Each method will produce fine macarons.

The easiest technique to master is the French meringue. After that the other techniques will seem easier.

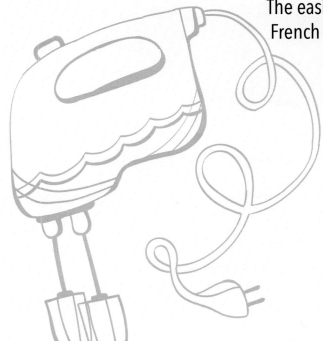

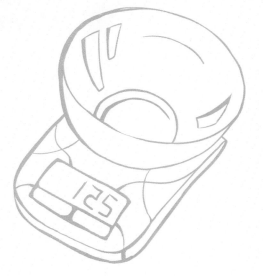

Finished Macarons,
French Meringue Technique

French Meringue Technique

French meringue is a combination of egg whites and raw sugar. This recipe makes a great base for creating your own flavors. Once you have mastered this macaron, look at the Macaron Flavoring chart on page 52 for instructions and inspiration.

EQUIPMENT:

1. Stand or Hand held mixer
2. Half baking trays lined with parchment or Silpats
3. Piping bag
4. Large bowl
5. Food processor
6. Flat rubber spatula
7. #12 Wilton tip or Ateco #803 or any plain round tip with a 3/8" diameter opening
8. Eye dropper – optional but good for adding color and flavor

INGREDIENTS:

227g Powdered Sugar
129g Almond Meal
129g Egg Whites
Pinch Cream of Tartar (⅛ tsp)
113g Granulated Sugar
½ tsp Vanilla Extract

French Meringue Macarons – Vanilla

Makes approximately 40-42 assembled cookies

Preheat oven to 325°F (conventional) 300 °F (convection).

1. Layer the powdered sugar and almond meal in a food processor or mini-prep fitted with a metal blade.

2. Pulse the powdered sugar and the almond meal in a food processor until the mixture looks like fine meal. This takes about 15 seconds or 8 pulses.

3. Using a stand or hand held mixer, whip the egg whites with the cream of tartar on medium speed until they look frothy and no egg white liquid remains. They will still have a yellowish cast and no structure.

4. With the mixer running, add the sugar slowly. Once the sugar is added turn the mixer on to medium high speed.

5. Continue to whip until the meringue is soft and shiny. At this stage it resembles "marshmallow fluff" and does not form a peak.

6. Stop the mixer and add color if desired and vanilla extract. Put the color on the bottom of the whisk or beater attachments.

7. Turn the mixer to high speed, whip the egg whites until the mixture begins to look dull and the lines of the whisk are visible on the surface of the meringue.

8. Now check for peak. The peak should be firm with the angle supporting the peak at 11:30. (see photo) Transfer to a medium sized bowl.

9. Fold in the almond meal and powdered sugar in three increments.

10. Paint the mixture halfway up the side of the bowl, using the flat side of your spatula. Then scrape the mixture down to the center of the bowl.

11. Repeat 2-3 times then check to see if the mixture slides slowly down the side of the bowl.

12. Pipe on parchment or Silpat lined baking sheets.

13. Slam the tray, hard, 4-6 times on the counter. Then fist bump each side of the tray twice.

14. Let dry until they look dull but not overly dry. **Drying time varies on humidity. In a dry climate the macarons can dry in 15-20 minutes and in a humid climate it can take 35-40 minutes. But never dry them for more than an hour.

15. While the macarons are drying, preheat the oven to 325°F, 170°C.

16. Place on the middle rack of the oven.

17. Check in 11 minutes.

18. If their tops slide then bake for 2 -3 more minutes. They should release from the parchment or Silpat without sticking. Check one or two. If they stick put them back in the oven for 1-2 more minutes.

19. Let them cool for a few minutes before removing from the Silpat or parchment paper.

Finished Macarons,
Swiss Meringue Technique

Swiss Meringue Technique

Swiss meringue is more stable and denser tharn French Meringue. Swiss meringue is characterized by heating the egg whites and granulated sugar to 120-160°F (49-70°C). This recipe also makes a great base for creating your own flavors. Once you have mastered this macaron, look at the Macaron Flavoring chart on page 52 for instructions and inspiration.

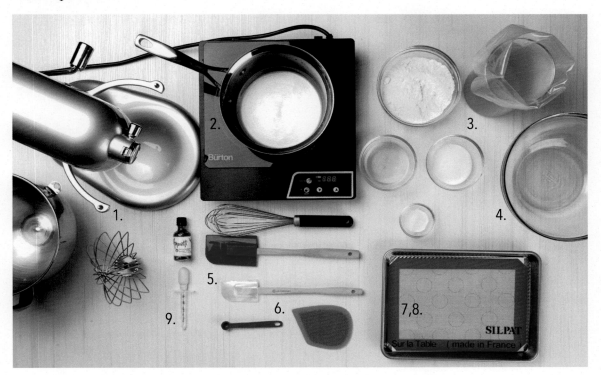

EQUIPMENT:
1. Stand or Hand held mixer
2. Saucepan for double boiler – the mixer bowl should rest on top of the saucepan not touch the water.
3. Piping bag
4. Large bowl
5. Flat rubber spatula
6. Bowl Scrapers
7. Parchment paper or Silpats and Templates
8. 2-3 Heavy Baking sheets
9. Eye dropper – optional but good for adding color and flavor
10. Food processor
11. #12 Wilton tip or Ateco #803 or any plain round tip with a 3/8" diameter opening

INGREDIENTS:
100g	Powdered Sugar
100g	Almond Meal
75g	Egg Whites
65g	Granulated Sugar
2-3	drops (no more than ½ teaspoon) Vanilla Extract

Swiss Meringue Macarons – Vanilla
Makes 22-25 cookies

Preheat oven to 325°F (conventional) 300 °F (convection).

1. Layer the powdered sugar and almond meal in a food processor or mini-prep fitted with a metal blade.

2. Pulse the powdered sugar and the almond meal in a food processor until the mixture looks like fine meal – about 15 seconds. Remove the dry mixture from the food processor and transfer to a bowl.

3. Place the egg whites, sugar and pinch of cream of tartar into the bowl of a stand mixer, whisk to combine. Make sure that the bowl and the whisk are impeccably clean.

4. Heat the egg whites and sugar to 120°F (49°C), whisk slowly as the mixture is heating.

5. Use an instant read or candy thermometer – if you don't have a thermometer the mixture should feel very warm to the touch.

6. Carefully attach the mixer bowl to the mixer.

7. Starting on medium speed whip the egg and cream of tartar until it looks like light foam. The egg whites should not appear liquid. The foam will be light and should not have any structure.

8. Continue to whip the meringue until it is soft and shiny. It should look like marshmallow fluff.

9. Now add the color and the few drops of extract.

10. Staying at medium high speed, whip the egg whites until they begins to dull and the lines of the whisk are visible on the surface of the meringue.

11. Now check for peak. The peak should be firm with the angle supporting the peak at 11:30. Transfer to a medium sized bowl.

12. Fold in the almond meal and powdered sugar in three increments.

13. Paint the mixture halfway up the side of the bowl, using the flat side of your spatula. Then scrape the mixture down to the center of the bowl.

14. Repeat 2-3 times then check to see if the mixture slides slowly down the side of the bowl.

15. Pipe on parchment or Silpat-lined baking sheets.

16. Slam the tray, hard, 4-6 times on the counter. Then fist bump each side of the tray twice.

17. Let dry until they look dull but not overly dry. ** Drying time varies on humidity. In a dry climate the macarons can dry in 15-20 minutes and in a humid climate it can take 35-40. But I never let them dry for over an hour.

18. While the macarons are drying, preheat the oven to 325°F, 160-170°C.

19. Place on the middle rack of the oven.

20. Check in 11 minutes.

21. If their tops slide, then bake for 2-3 more minutes. They should release from the parchment or Silpat without sticking. Check one or two. If they stick, put them back in the oven for 1-2 more minutes.

22. Let them cool for 10 minutes before removing from the Silpat or parchment paper.

Finished Macarons,
Italian Meringue Technique

Classic Italian Meringue Technique

Italian meringue is a cooked meringue that uses egg whites and a hot sugar syrup. It is very stable. This method is the most complicated but it is a nice challenge after you have mastered the rest.

EQUIPMENT:
1. Stand or Hand held mixer
2. Saucepan for cooking sugar
3. Large bowl
4. Piping bag
5. Eye dropper – optional but good for adding color and flavor
6. Colors – water soluble
7. Flat rubber spatula
8. Bowl Scrapers
10. Food processor
11. #12 Wilton tip or Ateco #803 or any plain round tip with a 3/8" diameter opening
12. 2-3 Heavy Baking sheets
13. Parchment paper, Silpats and templates

INGREDIENTS:
150g Powdered Sugar
150g Almond Meal
56g Egg Whites

45g Water
128g Granulated Sugar

57g Egg Whites
2-3 drops of Vanilla Extract

Classic Italian Meringue Macarons
Makes 30-35 cookies

Preheat oven to 325°F (conventional) 300°F (convection).

1. Layer the powdered sugar and almond meal in a food processor or mini-prep fitted with a metal blade.

2. Pulse the powdered sugar and the almond meal in a food processor until the mixture looks like fine meal – about 15 seconds or 8 pulses. Remove the dry mixture from the food processor and transfer to a bowl.

3. Combine the first amount of egg whites and the almond meal powdered sugar mixture into a medium sized bowl – stir well – it will be thick. The mixer with the paddle attachment can also be used. Mix for 30 seconds on medium low speed.

4. Place the remaining egg white in a clean mixer bowl fitted with the whisk attachment.

5. Turn the mixer on to medium - low speed, dropping the whisk to make sure that the whisk touches the eggs, if necessary

6. Place the water and sugar in a small saucepan – it should look like wet sand.

7. Bring to a boil over medium heat. It is a small amount of sugar and will cook quickly.

8. When the sugar reaches 230°F (110°C) add gel color.

9. At 236°F (113°C) remove from the heat and carefully pour the hot sugar into the moving egg whites. Lock the lip of the pot to the lip of the mixer bowl and aim for the space between the whisk and the bowl.

10. Turn the mixer to medium high and whip until the meringue cools to 94°F (34°C) meaning you can comfortably touch the side of the bowl.

11. Add the vanilla extract.

12. Now check for peak. The peak should be firm with the angle supporting the peak at 11:30. If the meringue is still soft, continue to mix on high speed until it is at medium peak.

13. Fold one third of the egg whites into the almond meal, sugar and egg white paste.

14. Fold in the rest.

15. Paint the mixture halfway up the side of the bowl, using the flat side of your spatula. Then scrape the mixture down to the center of the bowl.

16. Repeat 1-2 times then check to see if the mixture slides slowly down the side of the bowl. **Because of the mixing method, this step is shorter than in the other techniques.

17. Pipe on parchment or Silpat lined baking sheets.

18. Slam the tray, hard, 4-6 times on the counter. Then fist bump each side of the tray twice.

19. Let dry until they look dull but not overly dry. **Drying time varies on humidity. In a dry climate the macarons can dry in 15-20 minutes – in a humid climate it can take 35-40. But I never let them dry for over an hour.

20. While the macarons are drying, preheat the oven to 330°F (170°C).

21. Place on the middle rack of the oven.

22. Check in 11 minutes.

23. If their tops slide then bake for 2 -3 more minutes. They should release from the parchment or Silpat without sticking. Check one or two. If they stick put them back in the oven for 1-2 more minutes.

24. Let them cool for 10 minutes before removing from the Silpat or parchment paper.

Finished Macarons,
Hybrid Italian Meringue Technique

Hybrid Italian Meringue Technique

This technique may be a "Baking with Colette" original. I developed it for a macaron class in San Diego. The original recipe was coffee flavored and paired with a salted caramel filling. I left those ingredients in the recipe as optional. The salted caramel is in the chapter **Filling your Macarons**, on page 75.

EQUIPMENT:
1. Stand or Hand held mixer
2. Saucepan for double boiler – the mixer bowl should rest on top of the saucepan, not touching the water.
3. Large bowl
4. Piping bag
5. Flat rubber spatula
6. Bowl Scrapers
7. Food processor
8. #12 Wilton tip or Ateco #803 or any plain round tip with a 3/8" diameter opening
9. 2-3 Heavy Baking sheets
10. Parchment paper, Silpats and templates

INGREDIENTS:
125g Almond Meal
150g Powdered Sugar
1 tsp Espresso Powder *(optional)*

87g Egg Whites
¼ tsp Meringue Powder *(optional)*

57g Water
113g Sugar
½ tsp Vanilla or Coffee Extract
Brown Gel Food Color

Hybrid Italian Meringue Technique
Makes 30-35 cookies

Preheat oven to 325°F (conventional) 300 °F (convection).

1. Layer the powdered sugar and almond meal in a food processor or mini-prep fitted with a metal blade.

2. Pulse the powdered sugar and the almond meal in a food processor until the mixture looks like fine meal – about 15 seconds. Remove the dry mixture from the food processor and transfer to a bowl.

3. Place the egg whites and optional meringue powder in the mixer bowl fitted with the whisk attachment and turn the mixer on to medium low speed.

4. Place the water and sugar in a small saucepan – it should look like wet sand.

5. Bring to a boil over medium heat. It is a small amount of sugar and will cook quickly.

6. When the sugar reaches 230°F, add the gel color.

7. At 236°F remove from the heat and carefully pour the hot sugar into the moving egg whites. Lock the lip of the pot to the lip of the mixer bowl and aim for the space between the whisk and the bowl.

8. Turn the mixer to medium high and whip until the meringue cools to 94°F (meaning you can comfortably touch the side of the bowl).

9. Add the vanilla or coffee extract.

10. Now check for peak. The peak should be firm with the angle supporting the peak at 11:30. Transfer to a medium sized bowl.

11. Fold in the almond meal and powdered sugar in three increments.

12. Paint the mixture halfway up the side of the bowl, using the flat side of your spatula. Then scrape the mixture down to the center of the bowl.

13. Repeat 2-3 times then check to see if the mixture slides slowly down the side of the bowl.

14. Pipe on parchment- or Silpat-lined baking sheets.

15. Slam the tray, hard, 4-6 times on the counter. Then fist bump each side of the tray twice.

16. Let dry until they look dull but not overly dry. **Drying time varies on humidity. In a dry climate the macarons can dry in 15-20 minutes and in a humid climate it can take 35-40 minutes. But I never let them dry for over an hour.

18. While the macarons are drying, preheat the oven to 325°F,160- 170°C.

19. Place on the middle rack of the oven.

20. Check in 11 minutes.

21. If their tops slide, then bake for 2 -3 more minutes. They should release from the parchment or Silpat without sticking. Check one or two. If they stick put them back in the oven for 1-2 more minutes.

22. Let them cool for a few minutes before removing from the Silpat or parchment paper.

Finished Macarons,
Contemporary Egg White Powder Technique

Contemporary Egg White Powder Technique

This uses powdered egg white not fresh egg whites. I came across this technique in Jordi Puigvert's amazing pastry book, "Evolution".

EQUIPMENT:

1. Stand or Hand held mixer
2. Food processor
3. Parchment paper, Silpats and templates
4. 2-3 Heavy Baking sheets
5. Large bowl
6. Piping bag
7. #12 Wilton tip or Ateco #803 or any plain round tip with a 3/8" diameter opening
8. Bowl Scrapers
9. Flat rubber spatula
10. Instant-read or candy thermometer

INGREDIENTS:

125g Powdered Sugar
125g Almond Meal
43g Water
4g Egg White Powder

43g Water
4 g Egg White Powder

55g Water
125g Sugar
½ tsp (3g) Vanilla extract
Gel Color

Contemporary Macaron Technique

Makes 30-35 cookies

Preheat oven to 325°F (conventional) 300 °F (convection).

1. Pulse the powdered sugar and the almond meal in a food processor until it looks like fine meal – about 15 seconds.

2. Combine the water and egg white powder in the bowl of the stand mixer, fitted with the paddle attachment. Add the powdered sugar and almond meal.

3. Mix for 30 seconds on low speed and then 30 seconds on medium speed.

4. Transfer the mixture to another bowl and wash the mixer.

5. Place the second amount of water and egg white powder in the bowl of the stand mixer.

6. Mix for 2 minutes on low speed, dropping the whisk if the whisk is not making contact with the egg white mixture. Keep the mixer going at medium speed.

7. Place the water and sugar in a small sauce pan, it should have the consistency of wet sand at the beach.

8. Cook the sugar to 118°C, (244°F). Add the sugar to the moving egg whites. Pour slowly. Once all the sugar is added, turn the mixer up to high speed. Mix until the egg whites are lukewarm. Check for a firm peak.

9. Add 1/3 of the meringue to the almond meal, confectioner's sugar and egg white paste. Fold until they are combined.

10. Add the rest of the meringue.

11. Paint the mixture halfway up the side of the bowl, using the flat side of your spatula. Then scrape the mixture down to the center of the bowl.

12. Repeat 2-3 times then check to see if the mixture slides slowly down the side of the bowl

13. Pipe on parchment or Silpat lined baking sheets.

14. Slam the tray, hard, 4-6 times on the counter. Then fist bump each side of the tray twice.

15. Let dry until they look dull but not overly dry. **Drying time varies on humidity. In a dry climate the macarons can dry in 15-20 minutes and in a humid climate it can take 35-40 minutes. But I never let them dry for over an hour.

16. While the macarons are drying, preheat the oven to 330°F, 170°C .

17. Place on the middle rack of the oven.

18. Check in 11 minutes.

19. If their tops slide then bake for 2-3 more minutes. They should release from the parchment or Silpat without sticking. Check one or two. If they stick, put them back in the oven for 1-2 more minutes.

20. Let them cool for 10 minutes before removing from the Silpat or parchment paper.

 NOTES

Chocolate Macarons

Creating a chocolate macaron can be tricky. It is getting the proportion of cocoa powder correct that is challenging. Cocoa is acidic, and a drying agent, so it directly reacts with the other ingredients.

Colette's Chocolate Macarons with Raspberry Gelée Filling

Chocolate Macarons - Hybrid Italian Meringue Technique with Lemon Curd

EQUIPMENT:

1. Stand or Hand held mixer
2. Food processor
3. Large bowl
4. Parchment paper, Silpats and templates
5. 2-3 Heavy Baking sheets
6. Bowl Scraper
7. Flat rubber spatula
8. Eye dropper – optional but good for adding color and flavor
9. Piping bag
10. #12 Wilton tip or Ateco #803 or any plain round tip with a 3/8" diameter opening

INGREDIENTS:

109g	Powdered Sugar
98g	Almond Meal
15g	Dutch Process Cocoa Powder
90g	Egg Whites
⅛ tsp	Cream of Tartar
75g	Granulated Sugar
½ tsp	Vanilla or Chocolate Extract
Brown Gel Color - optional	

Colette's Chocolate Macarons - French Meringue Technique
Makes 30-35 cookies   (Note recipe may be cut in half)

Preheat oven to 325°F or 160°C (conventional), 300°F or 150°C (convection).

1. Layer the powdered sugar, almond meal and cocoa in a food processor or mini-prep fitted with a metal blade.

2. Pulse the powdered sugar and the almond meal in a food processor until the mixture looks like fine meal. This takes about 15 seconds or 8 pulses.

3. Using a stand or hand held mixer, whip the egg whites with the cream of tartar on medium speed until they look frothy and no egg white liquid remains. They will still have a yellowish cast and no structure.

4. With the mixer running, add the granulated sugar slowly. Once the sugar is added turn the mixer on to medium high speed.

5. Continue to whip until the meringue is soft and shiny. At this stage it resembles "marshmallow fluff" or "shaving cream" and does not form a peak.

6. Stop the mixer and add color if desired and extract. Put the color on the bottom of the whisk or beater attachments.

7. Turn the mixer to high speed, whip the egg whites until the mixture begins to look dull and the lines of the whisk are visible on the surface of the meringue.

8. Now check for peak. The peak should be firm with the angle supporting the peak at 11:30. Transfer to a medium sized bowl.

9. Fold in the almond meal, powdered sugar and cocoa in three increments.

10. Paint the mixture halfway up the side of the bowl, using the flat side of your spatula. Then scrape the mixture down to the center of the bowl.

11. Repeat 2-3 times then check to see if the mixture slides slowly down the side of the bowl.

12. Pipe on parchment- or Silpat-lined baking sheets.

13. Slam the tray, hard, 4-6 times on the counter. Then fist bump each side of the tray twice.

14. Let dry until they look dull but not overly dry. **Drying time varies on humidity. In a dry climate the macarons can dry in 15-20 minutes and in a humid climate it can take 35-40 minutes. But never dry them for more than an hour.

15. While the macarons are drying, preheat the oven to 325°F, 170°C.

16. Place on the middle rack of the oven.

17. Check in 11 minutes.

18. If their tops slide, then bake for 2 -3 more minutes. They should release from the parchment or Silpat without sticking. Check one or two. If they stick put them back in the oven for 1-2 more minutes.

19. Let them cool for a few minutes before removing from the Silpat or parchment paper.

EQUIPMENT:

1. Stand or Hand held mixer
2. Saucepan
3. 2-3 Heavy Baking sheets
4. Parchment paper, Silpats and templates
5. Flat rubber spatula
6. Large bowl
7. Piping bag
8. Bowl Scrapers
9. Food processor
10. #12 Wilton tip or Ateco #803 or any plain round tip with a 3/8" diameter opening

INGREDIENTS:

150g Almond Meal
150g Powdered Sugar
 23g Dutch Process Cocoa Powder

120g Egg Whites
¼ tsp Meringue Powder *(optional)*

 57g Water
158g Sugar
½ tsp Vanilla or Chocolate Extract
Red Gel Color - optional for Red
Velvet Macarons

Red Velvet/Chocolate Macarons - Hybrid Italian Meringue Technique

Makes 25 cookies   Note: recipe may be cut in half

Preheat oven to 325°F or 160°C (conventional), 300°F or 150°C (convection).

1. In a food processor or mini prep – grind the almond meal, powdered sugar and cocoa until it is a fine powder about 15 seconds, 8 pulses.

2. Place the egg whites and optional meringue powder in the mixer bowl fitted with the whisk attachment.

3. Place the water and sugar in a small saucepan – it should look like wet sand.

4. Bring to a boil over medium heat. It is a small amount of sugar and will cook quickly.

5. When the sugar reaches 230 degrees add the gel color. At 236°F remove from the heat and carefully pour the hot sugar into the moving egg whites. Lock the lip of the pot to the lip of the mixer bowl and aim for the space between the whisk and the bowl.

6. Turn the mixer to medium high and whip until the meringue cools to 94°F (meaning you can comfortably touch the side of the bowl).

7. Add the vanilla or chocolate extract and red color.

8. Turn the mixer to high speed, whip the egg whites until the mixture begins to look dull and the lines of the whisk are visible on the surface of the meringue.

9. Now check for peak. The peak should be firm with the angle supporting the peak at 11:30. Transfer to a medium sized bowl.

10. Fold in the almond meal, powdered sugar and cocoa mixture into the meringue in three increments.

11. Paint the mixture halfway up the side of the bowl, using the flat side of your spatula. Then scrape the mixture down to the center of the bowl.

12. Repeat 2-3 times then check to see if the mixture slides slowly down the side of the bowl.

13. Pipe on parchment- or Silpat-lined baking sheets.

14. Slam the tray, hard, 4-6 times on the counter. Then fist bump each side of the tray twice.

15. Let dry until they look dull but not overly dry. **Drying time varies on humidity. In a dry climate the macarons can dry in 15-20 minutes and in a humid climate it can take 35-40. But I never let them dry for over an hour.

16. While the macarons are drying, preheat the oven to 325°F,160-170°C.

17. Place on the middle rack of the oven.

18. Check in 11 minutes.

19. If their tops slide then bake for 2 -3 more minutes. They should release from the parchment or Silpat without sticking. Check one or two. If they stick put them back in the oven for 1-2 more minutes.

20. Let them cool for a few minutes before removing from the Silpat or parchment paper.

 NOTES

Savory & Nut-Free

French Meringue Technique works best for creating savory macarons. Making a good savory macaron shell is complicated because the macaron depends on sugar for structure. Here is a formula for a savory shell that is not too sweet and perfect when paired with a savory filling.

I am often asked if it is possible to make a nut-free macaron, now it is. There are two seeds that work: pumpkin and sunflower. Commercial seed meals have to be used for these macarons. There is too much oil in the seeds for the processing to be done at home.

*Savory Macarons - Bloody Mary shell with Cucumber Cream Cheese Filling**

* See recipe for filling on page 67

Savory Macarons

The savory macarons in the photographs are made with Amoretti® Bloody Mary Powder. The gel color used is Wilton Christmas Red. They are filled with a cream cheese and herb filling and thinly sliced cucumbers.

EQUIPMENT:
1. Stand or Hand held mixer
2. Food processor
3. Bowl Scraper
4. Large bowl
5. Piping bag
6. Flat rubber spatula
7. Parchment paper or Silpats, and templates
8. 2 Half Baking sheets
9. #12 Wilton tip or Ateco #803 or any plain round tip with a 3/8" diameter opening
10. Eye dropper – optional but good for adding color and flavor

INGREDIENTS:
150g Powdered Sugar
125g Almond Meal
100g Egg Whites
  3g Cream of Tartar (⅛ tsp)
 35g Granulated Sugar
½ tsp Worcestershire
Pinch of salt and pepper
Gel Color
Cucumber Cream Cheese Filling (see page 67)

Optional: 1 tsp freeze-dried vegetable powder, or Amoretti® Blood Mary Seasoning Extract Powder (#1282) as used here.

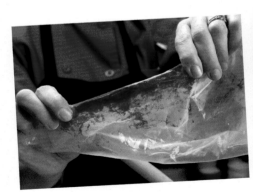

Savory Macarons - French Meringue Technique

Makes 30-35 cookies (Note: recipe may be cut in half)

Preheat oven to 325°F or 160°C (conventional) 300°F or 150°C (convection).

1. Layer the powdered sugar, almond meal and optional vegetable powder in a food processor or mini-prep fitted with a metal blade.

2. Pulse the powdered sugar and the almond meal in a food processor until the mixture looks like fine meal. This takes about 15 seconds or 8 pulses.

3. Using a stand or hand held mixer, whip the egg whites with the cream of tartar on medium speed until they look frothy and no egg white liquid remains. They will still have a yellowish cast and no structure.

4. With the mixer running, add the sugar slowly. Once the sugar is added turn the mixer on to medium high speed.

5. Continue to whip until the meringue is soft and shiny. At this stage it resembles "marshmallow fluff" and does not form a peak.

6. Stop the mixer and add Worcestershire sauce and salt and pepper. If adding color put it on the bottom of the whisk or beater attachments.

7. Turn the mixer to high speed, whip the egg whites until the mixture begins to look dull and the lines of the whisk are visible on the surface of the meringue.

8. Now check for peak. The peak should be firm with the angle supporting the peak at 11:30. Transfer to a medium sized bowl.

9. Fold in the almond meal and powdered sugar in three increments.

10. Paint the mixture halfway up the side of the bowl, using the flat side of your spatula. Then scrape the mixture down to the center of the bowl.

11. Repeat 2-3 times then check to see if the mixture slides slowly down the side of the bowl.

12. Stripe the seam of the piping bag with gel color before filling to achieve the marble effect shown in the photographs.

13. Pipe on parchment or Silpat lined baking sheets. Sprinkle tops with a little salt and pepper.

14. Slam the tray, hard, 4-6 times on the counter. Then fist bump each side of the tray twice.

15. Let dry until they look dull but not overly dry. **Drying time varies on humidity. In a dry climate the macarons can dry in 15-20 minutes and in a humid climate it can take 35-40 minutes. But never dry them for more than an hour.

16. While the macarons are drying, preheat the oven to 325°F (160°C).

17. Place on the middle rack of the oven.

18. Check in 11 minutes.

19. If their tops slide then bake for 2 -3 more minutes. They should release from the parchment or Silpat without sticking. Check one or two. If they stick put them back in the oven for 1-2 more minutes.

20. Let them cool for a few minutes before removing from the Silpat or parchment paper.

Pumpkin seed shells with a maple buttercream

Sunflower seed shells with dark chocolate ganache

Nut-free Macarons

I am often asked if it is possible to make a nut-free macaron, now it is. There are two seeds that work: pumpkin and sunflower. Commercial seed meals have to be used for these macarons, there is too much oil in the seeds for this to be done at home.

EQUIPMENT:

1. Stand or handheld mixer
2. Food processor
3. Piping bag
4. Parchment paper or Silpats, and templates
5. 2 Half baking sheets
6. Flat rubber spatula
7. Bowl scraper
8. Large bowl
9. Flat rubber spatula
10. #12 Wilton tip or Ateco #803 or any plain round tip with a 3/8″ diameter opening
11. Eye dropper – optional but good for adding color and flavor

INGREDIENTS:

198g Powdered Sugar
113g Pumpkin Seed or Sunflower Seed Meal
113g Egg Whites
3g Cream of Tartar (⅛ tsp)
100g Granulated Sugar
½ tsp Vanilla Extract
Extra pumpkin meal for dusting
Orange Gel Color

Nut-Free Macarons - French Meringue Technique
Makes 30-35 cookies (Note: recipe may be cut in half)

Preheat oven to 325°F or 160°C (conventional), 300°F or 150°C (convection).

1. Layer the powdered sugar and pumpkin seed meal in a food processor or mini-prep fitted with a metal blade.

2. Pulse the powdered sugar and the pumpkin seed meal in a food processor until the mixture looks like fine meal. This takes about 15 seconds or 8 pulses.

3. Using a stand or hand held mixer, whip the egg whites with the cream of tartar on medium speed until they look frothy and no egg white liquid remains. They will still have a yellowish cast and no structure.

4. With the mixer running, add the sugar slowly. Once the sugar is added turn the mixer on to medium high speed.

5. Continue to whip until the meringue is soft and shiny. At this stage it resembles "marshmallow fluff" and does not form a peak.

6. Stop the mixer and add color if desired and vanilla extract. Put the color on the bottom of the whisk or beater attachments.

7. Turn the mixer to high speed, whip the egg whites until the mixture begins to look dull and the lines of the whisk are visible on the surface of the meringue.

8. Now check for peak. The peak should be firm with the angle supporting the peak at 11:30. Transfer to a medium sized bowl.

9. Fold in the almond meal and powdered sugar in three increments.

10. Paint the mixture halfway up the side of the bowl, using the flat side of your spatula. Then scrape the mixture down to the center of the bowl.

11. Repeat 2-3 times then check to see if the mixture slides slowly down the side of the bowl.

12. Pipe on parchment or Silpat lined baking sheets. Dust with a little pumpkin meal if desired.

13. Slam the tray, hard, 4-6 times on the counter. Then fist bump each side of the tray twice (see photo).

14. Let dry until they look dull but not overly dry. **Drying time varies on humidity. In a dry climate the macarons can dry in 15-20 minutes and in a humid climate it can take 35-40 minutes. But never dry them for more than an hour.

15. While the macarons are drying, preheat the oven to 325°F (170°C).

16. Place on the middle rack of the oven.

17. Check in 11 minutes.

18. If their tops slide then bake for 2 -3 more minutes. They should release from the parchment or Silpat without sticking. Check one or two. If they stick put them back in the oven for 1-2 more minutes.

19. Let them cool for a few minutes before removing from the Silpat or parchment paper.

NOTES

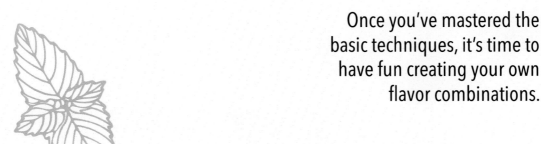

Customizing your Macaron Shells

Once you've mastered the basic techniques, it's time to have fun creating your own flavor combinations.

Strawberry Macarons with
Strawberry-Champagne Buttercream*

* See recipe for buttercream on page 79

Customizing your macarons with flavor and texture

Once you master the basic technique, you can start to get creative with your macarons. The trick is not to overdo it. A little flavor goes a long way.

Also, you must be very careful not to add anything to the shell that will throw off the chemistry of the batter, this includes ingredients that contain a lot of acid.

When adding extracts, liqueurs and "flavorings" – remember a little goes a long way.

Most extracts are suspended in water soluble mediums, typically alcohol. They are also very strong in flavor. Use an eye dropper when adding extracts, liqueurs and flavorings to the macaron shells.

Add no more then 2-3 drops for the base recipe. Too much extract and the shells will be super thin, delicate and almost translucent. This is because alcohol in the extract thins the egg white protein. If this happens, the finished macarons will have a very thin top.

Any oil based flavoring (including candy oils) will not work. The meringue will not whip up properly if any fat soluble product is added to it.

Freeze dried fruits, vegetables, dry spices and loose tea can be added to the almond meal and powdered sugar when you pulverize it in your food processor.

Process the added ingredient to a fine powder before adding it to the powdered sugar and almond meal mix. This keeps your finished shell smooth.

Leftover fruit powders and vegetables should be stored with desiccant, if possible.

Add no more than one teaspoon to the base recipe.

HOW TO GET STARTED

Choose a base recipe
(technique of your choice)

Add 1 teaspoon of:
Freeze dried fruit powder or vegetable powder, ground lavender, espresso powder, cinnamon, saffron, cardamom, etc added to the powdered sugar and almond meal in the food processor.

1/2 teaspoon
Extracts or liqueurs

Lavender shells with white chocolate ganache (pg 69)

Suggestions for Customizing –

MACARON SHELLS

BASE FLAVORS
- Vanilla
- Chocolate
- Coffee

FRUIT FLAVORS
Using freeze-dried fruit powder, extracts and flavorings:
- Apricot
- Banana
- Blueberry
- Peach
- Mango
- Raspberry
- Strawberry
- Lemon
- Lime
- Orange

HERBAL/TEA
- Lavender
- Mint
- Earl Gray

SPICES
- Cinnamon
- Cardamom
- Saffron
- Ginger

USING OTHER NUTS
½ of the total weight must be Almond Meal
- Cashew
- Hazelnut
- Macadamia
- Pecan
- Pistachio
- Walnut

SEEDS
- Pumpkin seeds/Pepitas
- Sunflower seeds

Successful combinations:

Strawberry Macarons · Yield 30-35 Macarons

EQUIPMENT:
Stand or handheld mixer
Large bowl
Food processor
Flat rubber spatula
Piping bag and #12 tip
2 half sheet trays, lined

INGREDIENTS:
198g Powdered Sugar
113g Almond Meal
1 tsp Freeze Dried Strawberries, ground
113g Egg Whites
3g Cream of Tartar (⅛ tsp)
100g Granulated Sugar
½ tsp Vanilla Extract, Red Gel Color

1. Pulse powdered sugar, almond meal, and strawberries in food processor, until the texture resembles fine meal.
2. Combine the egg whites with cream of tartar, whip on medium speed until frothy, rain in sugar, increase to medium high speed, add color and extract, and increase to high speed whip to firm peak.
3. Transfer to mixing bowl.
4. Fold in dry ingredients.
5. Paint and scrape.
6. Pipe and dry.
7. Bake at 325°F. Check in 11 minutes.

Lavender Macarons · Yield 30-35 Macarons

EQUIPMENT:
Stand or handheld mixer
Large bowl
Food processor
Flat rubber spatula
Piping bag and #12 tip
2 half sheet trays, lined

INGREDIENTS:
198g Powdered Sugar
113g Almond Meal
1 tsp Ground Dried Lavender
113g Egg Whites
3g Cream of Tartar (⅛ tsp)
100g Granulated Sugar
½ tsp Lavender Extract, Purple Gel Color

1. Pulse powdered sugar, almond meal, and lavender in food processor, until the texture resembles fine meal.
2. Combine the egg whites with cream of tartar, whip on medium speed until frothy, rain in sugar, increase to medium high speed, add color and extract, and increase to high speed whip to firm peak.
3. Transfer to mixing bowl.
4. Fold in dry ingredients.
5. Paint and scrape.
6. Pipe, sprinkle with lavender, and dry.
7. Bake at 325°F. Check in 11 minutes.

Rose Petal Macarons

These are lovely with a glass of dry sparkling wine – Champagne would be perfect. But I would be happy with Cava or Prosecco. In my macaron world, it doesn't get more romantic than this.

EQUIPMENT:

1. Stand or handheld mixer
2. Food processor
3. Piping bag
4. Parchment paper or Silpats
5. 2 Half baking sheets
6. Heart-shaped template
7. Flat rubber spatula
8. Large bowl
9. #12 Wilton tip or Ateco #803 or any plain round tip with a 3/8" diameter opening
10. Eye dropper – optional but good for adding color and flavor

INGREDIENTS:

198g Powdered Sugar
113g Almond Meal
1 tsp Dried Edible Rose Petals
(pre-grind in food processor)
113g Egg Whites
3g Cream of Tartar (⅛ tsp)
100g Granulated Sugar
½ tsp Vanilla Extract
3 drops Rose Extract or Rose Water
Red or Pink Gel Color
Extra rose petals for dusting
(pre-grind in food processor)

Rose Petal Macarons - French Meringue Technique

Makes 30-35 cookies (Note: recipe may be cut in half)

Preheat oven to 325°F or 160°C (conventional), 300°F or 150°C (convection).

1. Layer the powdered sugar, almond meal and pre-ground rose petals in a food processor or mini-prep fitted with a metal blade.

2. Pulse the powdered sugar and the almond meal in a food processor until the mixture looks like fine meal. This takes about 15 seconds or 8 pulses.

3. Using a stand or hand held mixer, whip the egg whites with the cream of tartar on medium speed until they look frothy and no egg white liquid remains. They will still have a yellowish cast and no structure.

4. With the mixer running, add the sugar slowly. Once the sugar is added turn the mixer on to medium high speed.

5. Continue to whip until the meringue is soft and shiny. At this stage it resembles "marshmallow fluff" and does not form a peak.

6. Stop the mixer and add color if desired, vanilla and rose extracts. Put the color on the bottom of the whisk or beater attachments.

7. Turn the mixer to high speed, whip the egg whites until the mixture begins to look dull and the lines of the whisk are visible on the surface of the meringue.

8. Now check for peak. The peak should be firm with the angle supporting the peak at 11:30. Transfer to a medium sized bowl.

9. Fold in the almond meal and powdered sugar in three increments.

10. Paint the mixture halfway up the side of the bowl, using the flat side of your spatula. Then scrape the mixture down to the center of the bowl.

11. Repeat 2-3 times then check to see if the mixture slides slowly down the side of the bowl.

12. Pipe on parchment or Silpat lined baking sheets. Sprinkle with extra crushed rose petals if desired.

13. Slam the tray, hard, 4-6 times on the counter. Then fist bump each side of the tray twice (see photo).

14. Let dry until they look dull but not overly dry. **Drying time varies on humidity. In a dry climate the macarons can dry in 15-20 minutes and in a humid climate it can take 35-40 minutes. But never dry them for more than an hour.

15. While the macarons are drying, preheat the oven to 325°F (170°C).

16. Place on the middle rack of the oven.

17. Check in 11 minutes.

18. If their tops slide then bake for 2 -3 more minutes. They should release from the parchment or Silpat without sticking. Check one or two. If they stick put them back in the oven for 1-2 more minutes.

19. Let them cool for a few minutes before removing from the Silpat or parchment paper.

Using <u>other</u> nut flavors to customize your macarons

Since the very beginning, macarons were made with almonds.

Almonds are the driest of all nuts and it makes sense to use them as a base for macarons. When other nuts are used in place of almonds, the excess oil from the nuts can form spots on the surface of the shell.

There is a way to make macarons using other kinds of nuts.

Replace half the almond meal with other nut meals.

Almost every nut will work. If the desired nut is available as a commercial meal, then use that.

If not, you'll need to make your own:

1. Nuts weigh the same whole as chopped so the first thing to do is weigh out the nuts.
2. Toast them at 350°F for 5-7 minutes. They should not take on color but instead the purpose of toasting them is to dry them out.
3. Cool them completely.
4. Rough chop by hand or machine, do not let them become oily at all.
5. Then process the partially ground or chopped nuts together with the almond meal and powdered sugar.

It's nice to garnish the tops of these macarons with a little sprinkle of finely chopped nuts, it highlights the ingredient and gives the macaron texture.

HOW TO GET STARTED

½ Almond Meal

+

½ Other Nut Meal
Examples include pistachio, walnut, hazelnut, cashew, macadamia or pecan.

+

Powdered Sugar

=

Alterna-nut Dry Mix

Walnut

Hazelnut

Pistachio

56

Alterna-nut Macarons

This macaron pairs well with the maple buttercream on page 76.

EQUIPMENT:

1. Stand or Hand held mixer
2. Food processor
3. Large bowl
4. Piping bag
5. Whisk
6. Flat rubber spatulas
7. Eye dropper – optional but good for adding color and flavor
8. Parchment paper, Silpats and templates
9. 2-3 Half sheet trays
10. #12 Wilton tip or Ateco #803 or any plain round tip with a 3/8" diameter opening

INGREDIENTS:

198g Powdered Sugar
57g Almond Meal
57g Pistachio, Walnut, Hazelnut, Cashew, Macadamia or Pecan Meal
113g Egg Whites
⅛ tsp Cream of Tartar
100g Granulated Sugar
½ tsp Vanilla Extract

Alterna-nut Macarons
Makes 30-35 cookies

Pistachio

Preheat oven to 325°F (conventional) 300 °F (convection).

1. Layer the powdered sugar, almond meal and other nut meal in a food processor or mini-prep fitted with a metal blade.

2. Pulse the powdered sugar and nut meals in a food processor until the mixture looks like fine meal. This takes about 15 seconds or 8 pulses.

3. Using a stand or hand held mixer, whip the egg whites with the cream of tartar on medium speed until they look frothy and no egg white liquid remains. They will still have a yellowish cast and no structure.

4. With the mixer running, add the sugar slowly. Once the sugar is added turn the mixer on to medium high speed.

5. Continue to whip until the meringue is soft and shiny. At this stage it resembles "marshmallow fluff" and does not form a peak.

6. Stop the mixer and add color if desired and vanilla extract. Put the color on the bottom of the whisk or beater attachments.

7. Turn the mixer to high speed, whip the egg whites until the mixture begins to look dull and the lines of the whisk are visible on the surface of the meringue.

8. Now check for peak. The peak should be firm with the angle supporting the peak at 11:30. Transfer to a medium sized bowl.

9. Fold in the almond meal and powdered sugar in three increments.

10. Paint the mixture halfway up the side of the bowl, using the flat side of your spatula. Then scrape the mixture down to the center of the bowl.

11. Repeat 2-3 times then check to see if the mixture slides slowly down the side of the bowl.

12. Pipe on parchment or Silpat lined baking sheets.

13. Slam the tray, hard, 4-6 times on the counter. Then fist bump each side of the tray twice.

14. Let dry until they look dull but not overly dry. **Drying time varies on humidity. In a dry climate the macarons can dry in 15-20 minutes and in a humid climate it can take 35-40 minutes. But never dry them for more than an hour.

15. While the macarons are drying, preheat the oven to 325°F, 170°C.

16. Place on the middle rack of the oven.

17. Check in 11 minutes.

18. If their tops slide then bake for 2 -3 more minutes. They should release from the parchment or Silpat without sticking. Check one or two. If they stick put them back in the oven for 1-2 more minutes.

19. Let them cool for a few minutes before removing from the Silpat or parchment paper.

 NOTES

Filling your Macarons

Now that your shells are finished, it's time to create some delicious fillings.

Suggestions for fillings -

FILLINGS

GANACHE

- Dark Chocolate
- Milk Chocolate
- White Chocolate

NOTE: The cream used in making ganache can be infused with herbs, spices, coffee and citrus. Liqueurs can also be added to ganache to create new flavors. Add liqueurs after the ganache is fully mixed.

BUTTERCREAM

Swiss Buttercream makes an ideal filling for macarons:

- Apricot
- Blueberry
- Cassis
- Champagne
- Cherry
- Chocolate
- Coffee
- Honey
- Lemon
- Mango
- Maple
- Raspberry
- Strawberry
- Vanilla

CARAMELS

- Classic Caramel
- Salted Caramel
- Chocolate Caramel

STORE-BOUGHT FILLINGS

(When you only have time for the shells.)

- Nutella
- Lemon curd
- Jam
- Marshmallow Fluff (or make your own - recipe on page 108)

Successful combinations:

Glossary of Fillings

Buttercream

Buttercream is a popular filling and icing. It is used to fill and mask cakes and to top cupcakes. It is easy to flavor and makes a delicious filling for macarons.

American and Swiss buttercreams are best suited for macaron fillings.

Caramel

Caramel is created from sugar that is cooked from 320-340°F. It ranges in color from light straw to deep amber. The addition of butter and cream transforms caramel from a hard candy to a soft delicious filling or confection.

Fruit Curds

Fruit Curds are sweet spreads used as fillings and toppings. Typically, they are made with citrus fruits. But other fruits can be used—mango, passion fruit, yuzu and raspberry are also popular.

Curds differ from pie fillings and custards in that they have a higher proportion of juice and zest.

They can also be folded into whipped cream, buttercream and ice cream base.

Ganache

Ganache is a mixture of chocolate and cream. Butter and flavorings are sometimes added for additional richness and flavor. Ganache can be used as a filling, an icing or a glaze. The proportion of cream and chocolate determines the consistency of the ganache. Ganache is a classic filling for macarons because it holds up well.

Gelées

Gelées are a mixture of fruit purée or juice, sugars and thickeners. Gelatin, agar agar and pectin are used to thicken gelées. A lightly sweetened gelée creates a nice flavor balance as macarons can be quite sweet.

Store-bought Fillings

Nutella, jam, commercial lemon curd and marshmallow fluff make credible fillings. If there is only enough time to make shells then it is fine to use one of the store-bought suggestions.

Dark Chocolate Ganache

Gelée

Notes on Gelées

Often in class, a student will ask me about those delicious fillings found in French macarons – the ones in France.

They have been described to me as a cross between good jam and a fruit roll-up.

Right away I know they are talking about gelées. Gelées are something the French do really well.

Gelées can be made with almost any juice or purée, fruit or vegetable. Sparkling wine can also be used. Gelées make interesting fillings for macarons as they are a nice change from jam. Also because vegetable juices and thin purées can be used, they are a nice choice for savory macarons.

Most gelée recipes call for large quantities of gelatin. The problem with this is that gelatin can soften at room temperature. I find that using a combination of gelatin and agar makes a stable gelée, one that stays firm even if the environment is warm.

There are two base recipes, one for sweet gelées and one for savory gelées. As you become more creative with your macaron fillings, you may have to taste the fruit or vegetable juice and adjust the sugar accordingly.

If you are using pineapple, kiwi, guava or papaya juice make sure it is heated to a minimum of 158°F or 70°C. These fruits contain bromelain which is an enzyme capable of digesting proteins. If unheated, the bromelain will break down the collagen in the gelatin. The result is a soupy mess.

ALL ABOUT AGAR

Agar is a polysaccharide that swells on contact with water. It should be dissolved in liquid that has been heated close to its boiling point.

2g of agar will thicken 500g of liquid.

Agar is extracted from red marine algae. It is used extensively in Asian desserts. It is a good choice for vegans. The gelées can be made with 100% agar.

Sources for agar:

- Amoretti.com
- Amazon.com

Sweet & Savory Gelées

The gelée recipes are all in grams – it is *essential* to use a scale to measure the agar.

EQUIPMENT:
1. Small baking pan (8 x 8")
   lined with plastic wrap
2. Saucepan
3. Whisk

SWEET GELÉE INGREDIENTS:
2g	Gelatin (1 sheet or ½ teaspoon powdered)
160g	Purée or Juice
38g	Sugar
2g	Agar

SAVORY GELÉE INGREDIENTS:
2g	Gelatin (1 sheet or ½ teaspoon powdered)
160g	Purée or Juice
10g	Sugar (more or less can be added depending on the sweetness of the purée)
2g	Agar

Sweet or Savory Gelée Base Technique

Gelée will keep for one week, covered, in the refrigerator.

1. Bloom the sheet gelatin by submerging it in very cold water for ten minutes until it softens. If using powdered gelatin, bloom it by sprinkling it over 2½ teaspoons of cold water – let it sit for 10 minutes.

2. Pour purée or juice into a saucepan. Add sugar.

3. Over medium heat, bring the mixture to a low boil and whisk in the agar. Let boil for one minute.

4. Remove from heat. Add gelatin.

5. Pour onto prepared pan and refrigerate until set.

Assembling macarons with gelées:

Use a small round cutter, slightly smaller than your macaron shells, to cut out circles of gelée. Transfer to shell with a small offset spatula.

Cucumber Cream Cheese Filling
Will keep for one week, covered in the refrigerator.

EQUIPMENT:
Medium bowl
Flat rubber spatula
Piping bag and #12 tip
or small offset spatula

INGREDIENTS:
6 oz Cream Cheese, softened
2 Green Onions, finely minced
¼ Cucumber, peeled & seeded,
finely chopped
Salt & Pepper, to taste

1. Combine cream cheese, green onion, and cucumber in a mixing bowl. Season with salt and pepper, mixing with a spatula until smooth.
2. Taste and adjust seasoning.
3. Pipe or spread onto shells.

→ This filling perfectly complements the savory Blood Mary shells on page 47.

Chocolate Ganache

Infuse the cream used in making ganache with herbs, spices, coffee or citrus.
Liqueurs can also be added to finished ganache to create new flavors.

EQUIPMENT:

1. Heatproof bowl
2. Saucepan
3. Spatula
4. Small baking pan (8 x 8")
   lined with plastic wrap

Dark Chocolate Ganache

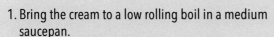

INGREDIENTS:
- 4 oz Semi-sweet Chocolate
- 4 oz Heavy Cream
- 1-2 tsp Extract or Liqueur (optional)

1. Bring the cream to a low rolling boil in a medium saucepan.
2. Place the chocolate in a heatproof bowl.
3. Pour the hot cream over the chocolate.
4. Let sit for 2-3 minutes and then stir with a spatula until the ganache is smooth. It should look glossy and rich.
5. Add optional extract or liqueur.
6. Pour the ganache on the plastic-lined tray. Cover with plastic wrap and refrigerate until set.

Milk or White Chocolate Ganache

INGREDIENTS:
- 4 oz Milk or White Chocolate
- 4 oz Heavy Cream
- 1-2 tsp Extract or Liqueur (optional)

1. Place the milk chocolate in a heatproof bowl.
2. Bring the cream up to a rolling boil.
3. Pour the hot cream over the chocolate and let sit for 15 seconds.
4. Stir with a spatula until smooth.
5. If the chocolate has not fully melted then place over a double boiler (the water should be steaming but the heat should be off) for a minute or two and stir again until the chocolate is fully melted.
6. Add extract or liqueur.
7. Pour onto plastic-lined tray, cover with a piece of plastic wrap and refrigerate until set.

MICROWAVE METHOD

1. Melt the chocolate in the microwave using 30 second intervals.
2. Heat the cream to a very low boil, remove from heat and add to the melted chocolate.
3. Stir with a spatula until smooth.
4. Add extract or liqueur.

Lemon Curd

Sweet, tart and utterly irresistible.

EQUIPMENT:
1. Saucepan
2. Whisk
3. Spatula
4. Strainer

INGREDIENTS:
4oz Fresh Lemon Juice
1   Lemon, zested
6oz Granulated Sugar
4   Egg Yolks
1   Egg
2oz Unsalted Butter, at room temperature
1tsp Powdered Gelatin
5tsp Cold Water, in a small bowl

Lemon Curd Technique

Store covered in the refrigerator for up to one week.

1. Sprinkle powdered gelatin* over the water, put aside until it sets up.

2. In the saucepan combine the lemon juice, zest, sugar, egg yolks, and egg.

3. Cook over medium heat until the mixture begins to thicken. It should never boil.

4. When the initial foam from mixing begins to subside and steam wafts off the surface, the curd is done. It will also coat the back of a wooden spoon. The temperature of the finished curd will be 180°F.

5. Strain the curd into a clean bowl. Stir in the bloomed gelatin and butter.

6. Cool over an ice bath then pour into plastic lined pan. Store covered in the refrigerator.

To substitute sheet gelatin for powdered, use 2 sheets and submerge in ice water until softened, about 10 minutes. To use, squeeze out excess water and add to hot lemon curd after straining in Step 5.

Classic Caramel

This is so delicious. At room temperature, use it to fill macarons.
Warmed, pour over ice cream.

EQUIPMENT:
1. Candy thermometer
2. 8 x 8" or small baking pan
3. Medium saucepan
4. Heat proof spatula

INGREDIENTS:
57g	Water
198g	Sugar
234g	Light Corn Syrup
¼ tsp	Salt
57g	Butter, cubed
8 oz	Heavy Cream
198g	Condensed Milk
14g	Amoretti® Vanilla

Classic Caramel Technique

Yields about 1¼ pounds (567g) caramel.

1. Line a small baking pan (8 x 8") with buttered parchment paper, making sure the edges of the paper extend over the top of the pan.

2. In the saucepan combine water, sugar, corn syrup, and salt. Clip the candy thermometer to the side of the pot, making sure it is not touching the bottom of the pan.

3. Bring to a boil over medium heat, do not stir, and boil until it reaches 250°F.

4. Reduce heat and add the butter. Once it has melted, add ½ cup of heavy cream. Be careful as the hot caramel will bubble up when the cream is added.

5. Keep at a low boil for 5 minutes then add remaining cream. Continue to boil until it reaches 250°F, stirring occasionally.

6. Add condensed milk and cook until it reaches 240°F, stirring constantly.

7. Remove from heat and add vanilla. Stir to combine.

8. Pour into prepared pan. Let it set up at room temperature. It will have a spreading or piping consistency. Once cool, cover and store at room temperature.

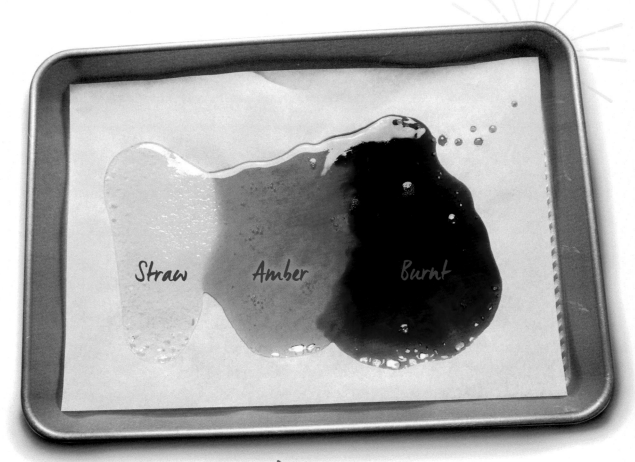

Straw   Amber   Burnt

CARAMEL TIPS

Use a saucepan with tall sides, as caramel rises significantly when additional ingredients are added.

Stay focused – avoid distractions when cooking sugar.

To avoid overcooking your caramel, have a bowl of cold water (larger than your pot!) nearby. Submerge the pot in the cold water to stop cooking.

To fill macaron shells with caramel, use a piping bag or spread with a small offset spatula.

Chocolate Caramel Filling

Yields 8 oz (227g). It will keep for one week in the refrigerator.

EQUIPMENT:
Medium saucepan
Heat proof spatula

INGREDIENTS:
28g Water
99g Sugar
14g Corn Syrup
170g Semi-sweet or Bittersweet Chocolate, chopped finely
1 tsp Vanilla Extract

1. Add the water to the saucepan, carefully pour the sugar into the middle of the pan, top with corn syrup. The mixture should have the consistency of wet sand at the beach.
2. Over medium heat bring the mixture to a boil, the sugar will dissolve. Cook until the sugar begins to change color, becoming straw color around the outside edge. Carefully swirl the pot to equalize the color.
3. Continue to cook until the sugar is a medium amber color.
4. Remove from heat and carefully add the heavy cream. Stir until combined.
5. Let sit for 2 minutes, stir in chocolate and vanilla.
6. Pour into a heatproof container. It will thicken as it cools and may be refrigerated to quickly cool and thicken.

Salted Caramel Filling

Yields about 8 oz, enough to fill about 30 macarons. Best if made the day before.

EQUIPMENT:
Candy thermometer
8x8" or small baking pan
Medium saucepan
Heat proof spatula

INGREDIENTS:
57g Water
255g Sugar
15g Light Corn Syrup (optional)
113g Crème Fraiche or Sour Cream
85g Butter, cubed
1 tsp Vanilla Extract
½ -1 tsp Fleur de Sel or Maldon sea salt

1. Line a small baking pan (8 x 8") with buttered parchment paper, making sure the edges of the paper extend over the top of the pan.
2. In the saucepan combine water, sugar, and optional corn syrup. Cook the mixture until it turns a medium amber color.
3. Add the crème fraiche or sour cream (watch for sugar splashes) and butter. Clip the candy thermometer to the side of the pot, making sure it is not touching the bottom of the pan.
4. Cook until the caramel reaches 245°F.
5. Remove from heat. Add vanilla and salt.
6. Pour into prepared pan and let cool, uncovered. Once cooled, cover and let sit overnight. It will set up to a filling consistency.

Leftover filled macarons will need to be refrigerated.

American Buttercream

American buttercream holds up better than any of the other buttercreams here. It is a good choice if refrigerating your macarons is not an option or if they are going to be part of a showpiece.

The trick to making American buttercream great is to mix it on medium-high speed for four minutes after all the ingredients are incorporated. This makes it smooth and light without adding a lot of air.

EQUIPMENT:
1. Stand mixer, fitted with the paddle attachment
2. Spatula

INGREDIENTS:
4 oz Butter, room temperature
8 oz Powdered Sugar
¼ tsp Salt
2 tsp Amoretti® Vanilla

1. Put the butter in the mixer bowl. Mix on low speed for one minute, increase speed to medium and mix another two minutes.

2. Stop the mixer and add half the sugar. Mix on low speed until the sugar is incorporated, then mix on medium speed for two minutes.

3. Add the remaining sugar. Mix on low speed until the sugar is incorporated, then mix on medium speed for two minutes

4. Add the vanilla and mix on medium high speed for four minutes.

This buttercream will keep in the refrigerator for one week and in the freezer for one month.

Thaw overnight in the refrigerator and beat on medium speed before using.

MAPLE VARIATION: Add 1 tbsp Pure Maple Syrup or 1 tsp Amoretti® Maple Extract W.S.

Swiss Buttercream

This recipe is a blank canvas; you can add any flavoring provided it is not too acidic. Swiss buttercream has a lovely texture and can be used anytime you need buttercream.

It is important to make sure the egg white mixture reaches 150°F to make the buttercream food safe.

EQUIPMENT:
1. Stand or hand held mixer, fitted with whisk attachment
2. Medium saucepan
3. Whisk
4. Spatula
5. Instant read thermometer

INGREDIENTS:
4 oz Egg whites
8 oz Granulated Sugar
8 oz Butter, cubed & chilled
2 tsp Amoretti® Vanilla

Swiss Buttercream Technique

1. Place egg whites and sugar in mixer bowl.

2. Set bowl over a medium saucepan filled a third of the way with simmering water (the bottom of the mixer bowl should not touch the water).

3. Whisk gently on medium heat until the mixture registers 150°F on an instant read thermometer.

4. Remove the bowl from the heat and attach it the stand mixer. If using a hand mixer – make sure the bowl is stable.

5. Whisk on high speed until the bowl no longer feels warm. It will look thick and marshmallow-like in texture.

6. Reduce speed to medium high. Add the butter one piece at a time – adding each additional piece as the previous one disappears.

7. When all the butter is added and the mixture looks fluffy and well emulsified – change to the paddle attachment.

8. On low speed add in the vanilla and mix until combined.

Strawberry Champagne Buttercream - Swiss Buttercream Technique

Refrigerate for up to five days or freeze up to one month.
Leftover filled macarons should be refrigerated.

EQUIPMENT:
Stand or hand held mixer
(fitted with whisk attachment)
Medium saucepan
Whisk
Instant read thermometer

INGREDIENTS:
2 oz Egg Whites
5 oz Granulated Sugar
8 oz Butter, cubed & chilled
1 tsp Vanilla Bean Paste
 (or ½ Vanilla Bean scraped + ½ tsp Vanilla Extract)
2 tsp Amoretti® Strawberry Champagne Extract #1228
Pink Food Color, optional
Garnish with freeze-dried or fresh strawberries

1. Place egg whites and sugar in mixer bowl.
2. Set bowl over a medium saucepan filled 1/3rd of the way with simmering water (the bottom of the mixer bowl should not touch the water).
3. Whisk on medium heat for 3-4 minutes or until the mixture registers 160°F on an instant read thermometer.
4. Remove the bowl from the heat and attach it the stand mixer. If using a hand mixer – make sure the bowl is stable.
5. Whisk on medium high speed until the mixture is at room temperature, 4-6 minutes.
6. Add the butter one piece at a time – adding each additional piece as the previous one disappears.
7. When all the butter is added and the mixture looks fluffy and well emulsified – change to the paddle attachment.
8. On low speed add in the vanilla, strawberry extract and optional pink color.

BUTTERCREAM TIPS

Store at room temperature 24 hours, refrigerate up to 5 days, and freeze up to one month. Thaw frozen buttercream in the refrigerator.

TO RECONSTITUTE:
Place buttercream in the mixer fitted with the paddle attachment. Mix on medium-high speed until fluffy and spreadable.

 NOTES

Macaron Cakes

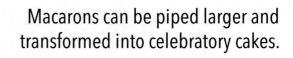

Macarons can be piped larger and transformed into celebratory cakes.

Black Forest Macaron Cake

COMPONENTS:

Chocolate Macaron Disks (plus 5-6 chocolate macaron halves)
Devil's Food Sponge cut into 6" circles
Kirsch Simple Syrup
Kirsch Chantilly Cream
1-2 oz Melted semisweet chocolate (to adhere small macarons to large shells)
5-6 Maraschino cherries with stems - dried off

EQUIPMENT:

1. Stand or handheld mixer
2. Food processor
3. Instant read thermometer
4. Piping bag
5. Parchment paper or Silpats
6. 1 Half baking sheet
7. Flat rubber spatula
8. Large bowl
9. #12 Wilton tip or Ateco #803 or any plain round tip with a 3/8" diameter opening

INGREDIENTS:

150g	Powdered Sugar
150g	Almond Meal
23g	Dutch Process Cocoa Powder
120g	Egg Whites
¼ tsp	Meringue Powder (optional)
158g	Granulated Sugar
57g	Water (2oz)
½ tsp	Vanilla or Chocolate Extract

Chocolate Macaron Disks

Yield: Two 6" macaron shells. Serves 5-6.

Preheat oven to 325°F or 160°C (conventional), 300°F or 150°C (convection).

1. Line the bottom of a half sheet tray with a piece of parchment paper. Draw two 6" circles on the paper and turn it over so that the ink or pencil does not bleed onto the macaron. A Silpat can be used on top of the template.

2. Layer the powdered sugar, almond meal and cocoa powder in a food processor or mini-prep fitted with a metal blade and process until the mixture looks like fine meal. This takes about 15 seconds or 8 pulses.

3. Using a stand or hand mixer, whip the egg whites and optional meringue powder on medium speed until they look frothy and no egg white liquid remains.

4. Meanwhile, bring the sugar and water to a boil over medium heat. At 236°F remove from the heat and carefully pour the hot sugar into the moving egg whites. Lock the lip of the pot to the lip of the mixer bowl and aim for the space between the whisk and the bowl.

5. Turn on the mixer to medium high and whip until the meringue cools to 94°F (you can comfortably touch the side of the bowl).

6. Stop the mixer and add chocolate or vanilla extract.

7. Turn the mixer to high speed, whip the egg whites until the mixture begins to look dull and the lines of the whisk are visible on the surface of the meringue.

8. Now check for peak. The peak should be firm with the angle supporting the peak at 11:30. Transfer to a medium sized bowl.

9. Fold in the almond meal, powdered sugar and cocoa mixture in three increments.

10. Paint the mixture halfway up the side of the bowl, using the flat side of your spatula. Then scrape the mixture down to the center of the bowl.

11. Repeat 2-3 times then check to see if the mixture slides slowly down the side of the bowl.

12. Pipe on parchment or Silpat lined baking sheets. Start piping in the center of the circle.

13. Slam the tray, hard, 4-6 times on the counter. Then fist bump each side of the tray twice.

14. Let dry until they look dull but not overly dry. **Drying time varies on humidity. In a dry climate the macarons can dry in 15-20 minutes and in a humid climate it can take 35-40 minutes. But never dry them for more than an hour.

15. While the macarons are drying, preheat the oven to 325°F, 170°C.

16. Place on the middle rack of the oven.

17. Check in 14 minutes.

18. If their tops slide then bake for 2-3 more minutes. They should release from the parchment or Silpat without sticking. Check one. If it sticks put them back in the oven for 1-2 more minutes.

19. Let them cool for a few minutes before removing from the Silpat or parchment paper.

• Devil's Food Sponge

Yield: Two 6" rounds. Any extra cake freezes beautifully.

EQUIPMENT:
Stand mixer fitted with whisk attachment
Quarter sheet pan or 9 x 13" pan
Parchment paper
Spatula
2 Medium bowls

INGREDIENTS:

133g	Cake Flour	113g	Coffee
43g	Cocoa Powder	170g	Sugar
4g	Baking Soda	64g	Eggs
2g	Fine Sea Salt	1 tsp	Vanilla Extract
99g	Buttermilk		
99g	Canola Oil		

1. Preheat the oven to 350°F.

2. Grease the pan and line the bottom with a piece of parchment paper.

3. In a medium bowl, sift together flour, cocoa powder, baking soda, and salt.

4. In the other medium bowl, combine the buttermilk, oil and coffee. It is ok if it separates.

5. Place egg, sugar and vanilla in mixer bowl and mix at low speed for 1 minute.

6. Stop the mixer and scrap down the sides. Increase mixer to medium speed and mix for 3 minutes.

7. Add flour mixture in three increments, alternating with the buttermilk mixture, starting and ending with the flour. Scrape down the bowl after each addition and mix just long enough to incorporate the flour. Do not overmix. This batter is loose.

8. Pour batter into prepared pan.

9. Bake for 22 minutes. Check for doneness by inserting a skewer or cake tester into the middle of the cake. If the skewer is wet, return the cake to the oven for an additional 5-7 minutes.

The Black Forest is in Germany, making this Italian-style French dessert truly international!

Kirsch Simple Syrup

EQUIPMENT:
Small saucepan
Whisk or spoon
Pastry brush

INGREDIENTS:
133g Water
133g Granulated Sugar
2 tsp Amoretti® Kirsch Extract

1. Bring water and sugar to a boil, stirring to dissolve sugar.

2. Once the sugar has dissolved and the syrup looks clear, remove pan from heat. Set aside to cool.

3. Add extract when syrup has cooled.

Refrigerated, syrup will keep 6 months.

Kirsch Chantilly Cream

EQUIPMENT:
Large bowl
Whisk or stand mixer fitted with whisk attachment

INGREDIENTS:
227g Heavy Cream
43g Powdered Sugar, sifted
1-2 tsp Amoretti® Kirsch Extract

1. Using the whisk or mixer, whip the cream until it is the consistency of yogurt.

2. Add sugar and extract.

3. Taste and adjust for sweetness.

4. Continue whipping until stiff peaks form.

Black Forest Macaron Cake *Assembly*

EQUIPMENT:
8" cardboard cake round
Spoon
Pastry brush
Piping bag
Medium star tip (824 or 825)

1. If sponge is thick, trim top with a serrated knife.

2. Starting ½" from the edge, carefully hollow out the top ¼" of the sponge (see photo).

3. Place one macaron disk on the cardboard cake round and carefully slide the hollowed sponge on top of the macaron disk.

4. With the pastry brush, soak the sponge with kirsch simple syrup.

5. Fill piping bag, fitted with the star tip, with kirsch chantilly cream.

6. Pipe a layer of chantilly cream on the sponge, starting in the center and finishing with a layer over the outer rim of the cake.

7. Top with remaining macaron disk.

8. Evenly space 5-6 macaron halves around the top disk, flat side up, using the melted chocolate to adhere them.

9. Pipe a big rosette of chantilly cream on each open macaron half and top each one with a maraschino cherry.

Red Velvet Macaron Cake

COMPONENTS:
Red Velvet Macaron Disks
Red Velvet Sponge cut into 6" circles
Cream Cheese Icing
Powdered sugar for dusting

EQUIPMENT:
1. Stand or handheld mixer
2. Food processor
3. Instant read thermometer
4. Piping bag
5. Parchment paper or Silpats
6. 1 Half baking sheet
7. Flat rubber spatula
8. Large bowl
9. #12 Wilton tip or Ateco #803 or any plain round tip with a 3/8" diameter opening

INGREDIENTS:
150g	Powdered Sugar
150g	Almond Meal
23g	Dutch Process Cocoa Powder
120g	Egg Whites
¼ tsp	Meringue Powder (optional)
158g	Granulated Sugar
57g	Water (2oz)
drop	Red Gel Color
½ tsp	Vanilla or Chocolate Extract

• Red Velvet Macaron Disks

Yield: Two 6" macaron shells. Serves 5-6.

Preheat oven to 325°F or 160°C (conventional), 300°F or 150°C (convection).

1. Line the bottom of a half sheet tray with a piece of parchment paper. Draw two 6" circles on the paper and turn it over so that the ink or pencil does not bleed onto the macaron. A silpat can be used on top of the template.

2. Layer the powdered sugar, almond meal and cocoa powder in a food processor or mini-prep fitted with a metal blade and process until the mixture looks like fine meal. This takes about 15 seconds or 8 pulses.

3. Using a stand or hand mixer, whip the egg whites and optional meringue powder on medium speed until they look frothy and no egg white liquid remains.

4. Meanwhile, bring the sugar and water to a boil over medium heat. When the mixture reaches 230°F, add the gel color. At 236°F remove from the heat and carefully pour the hot sugar into the moving egg whites. Lock the lip of the pot to the lip of the mixer bowl and aim for the space between the whisk and the bowl.

5. Turn on the mixer to medium high and whip until the meringue cools to 94°F (you can comfortably touch the side of the bowl).

6. Stop the mixer and add chocolate or vanilla extract.

7. Turn the mixer to high speed, whip the egg whites until the mixture begins to look dull and the lines of the whisk are visible on the surface of the meringue.

8. Now check for peak. The peak should be firm with the angle supporting the peak at 11:30. Transfer to a medium sized bowl.

9. Fold in the almond meal, powdered sugar and cocoa mixture in three increments.

10. Paint the mixture halfway up the side of the bowl, using the flat side of your spatula. Then scrape the mixture down to the center of the bowl.

11. Repeat 2-3 times then check to see if the mixture slides slowly down the side of the bowl.

12. Pipe on parchment or Silpat lined baking sheets. Start piping in the center of the circle.

13. Slam the tray, hard, 4-6 times on the counter. Then fist bump each side of the tray twice.

14. Let dry until they look dull but not overly dry. **Drying time varies on humidity. In a dry climate the macarons can dry in 15-20 minutes and in a humid climate it can take 35-40 minutes. But never dry them for more than an hour.

15. While the macarons are drying, preheat the oven to 325°F, 170°C.

16. Place on the middle rack of the oven.

17. Check in 14 minutes.

18. If their tops slide then bake for 2 -3 more minutes. They should release from the parchment or Silpat without sticking. Check one. If it sticks put them back in the oven for 1-2 more minutes.

19. Let them cool for a few minutes before removing from the Silpat or parchment paper.

• Red Velvet Sponge

Yield: Two 6" rounds. Any extra cake freezes beautifully.

EQUIPMENT:
Stand mixer fitted with the whisk attachment
Quarter sheet pan or 13 x 9" pan
Parchment paper
Spatula

INGREDIENTS:

221g	Cake Flour	14g	Red Gel Color
52g	Cocoa Powder	1 tsp	Vanilla Extract
2g	Fine Sea Salt	142g	Buttermilk
176g	Canola Oil	1 tsp	Baking Soda
272g	Sugar	1¼ tsp	White Vinegar
74g	Eggs		

1. Preheat oven to 350°F.

2. Brush the sides and bottom of the quarter sheet pan or 13 x 9" pan with vegetable oil or spray with pan spray. Line the bottom with a piece of parchment paper.

3. Sift flour, cocoa powder and salt together.

4. Place oil, sugar and vanilla in mixer bowl and mix at medium speed for 2 minutes.

5. Add eggs and vanilla. Mix for 2 minutes in medium high speed. The mixture will be thick and pale yellow in color.

6. Turn the mixer off, add the color. Turn the mixer to low and mix for one minute until color is incorporated.

7. Add flour and cocoa mixture alternately with buttermilk. Starting with dry ingredients and ending with dry ingredients. Scrape down the bowl after each addition and mix just long enough to incorporate the ingredients. Do not overmix.

8. Place the baking soda in a small dish, add the vinegar. Add to the batter. Mix for 10 seconds on medium speed.

9. Pour batter into prepared pans.

10. Bake for 30 minutes and check for doneness by inserting a skewer or cake tester into the middle of the cake. If the skewer is wet, return the cake to the oven for an additional 5-7 minutes.

• Cream Cheese Icing

Cream cheese icing will keep for one week in the refrigerator, one month in the freezer.

EQUIPMENT:
Stand mixer fitted with paddle attachment
Spatula

INGREDIENTS:
133g Butter, softened
227g Cream Cheese, softened
1 tsp Vanilla Extract
340g Powdered Sugar, sifted

1. In the mixer bowl, combine butter and cream cheese. Mix on low speed 1 minute.

2. Scrape down the bowl and add vanilla.

3. Increase the mixer speed to medium and mix for 3 minutes. Scrape down the bowl.

4. Add powdered sugar in three increments, starting on low speed and increasing speed to medium. Mix for 3 minutes before adding the next increment of sugar. Repeat until all the sugar has been added.

Red Velvet Macaron Cake *Assembly*

EQUIPMENT:
8" cardboard cake round
Spoon
Piping bag
Medium star tip (824 or 825)

1. If sponge is thick, trim top with a serrated knife.

2. Starting ½" from the edge, carefully hollow out the top ¼" of the sponge (see photo).

3. Place one macaron disk on the cardboard cake round and carefully slide the hollowed sponge on top of the macaron disk.

4. Fill piping bag, fitted with the star tip, with cream cheese icing.

5. Pipe a layer of cream cheese icing on the sponge, starting in the center and finishing with a layer over the outer rim of the cake.

6. Top with remaining macaron disk.

7. Sprinkle with powdered sugar to garnish.

Boston Cream Pie Macaron Cake

COMPONENTS:

Vanilla Macaron Disks
Vanilla Sponge cut into 6" circles
Vanilla Simple Syrup
Pastry Cream
Ganache

EQUIPMENT:

1. Stand or handheld mixer
2. Food processor
3. Instant read thermometer
4. Piping bag
5. Parchment paper or Silpats
6. 1 Half baking sheet
7. Flat rubber spatula
8. Large bowl
9. #12 Wilton tip or Ateco #803 or any plain round tip with a 3/8" diameter opening

INGREDIENTS:

198g	Powdered sugar
113g	Almond meal
113g	Egg whites
⅛ tsp	Cream of tartar
100g	Granulated sugar
½ tsp	Vanilla extract

• Vanilla Macaron Disks

Yield: Two 6" macaron shells. Serves 5-6.

Preheat oven to 325°F or 160°C (conventional), 300°F or 150°C (convection).

1. Line the bottom of a half sheet tray with a piece of parchment paper. Draw two 6" circles on the paper and turn it over so that the ink or pencil does not bleed onto the macaron. A silpat can be used on top of the template.

2. Layer the powdered sugar and almond meal in a food processor or mini-prep fitted with a metal blade.

3. Pulse the powdered sugar and the almond meal in a food processor until the mixture looks like fine meal. This takes about 15 seconds or 8 pulses.

4. Using a stand or hand held mixer, whip the egg whites with the cream of tartar on medium speed until they look frothy and no egg white liquid remains. They will still have a yellowish cast and no structure.

5. With the mixer running, add the sugar slowly. Once the sugar is added turn the mixer on to medium high speed.

6. Continue to whip until the meringue is soft and shiny. At this stage it resembles "marshmallow fluff" and does not form a peak.

7. Stop the mixer and add vanilla extract.

8. Turn the mixer to high speed, whip the egg whites until the mixture begins to look dull and the lines of the whisk are visible on the surface of the meringue.

9. Now check for peak. The peak should be firm with the angle supporting the peak at 11:30. Transfer to a medium sized bowl.

10. Fold in the almond meal and powdered sugar in three increments.

11. Paint the mixture halfway up the side of the bowl, using the flat side of your spatula. Then scrape the mixture down to the center of the bowl.

12. Repeat 2-3 times then check to see if the mixture slides slowly down the side of the bowl.

13. Pipe on parchment or Silpat lined baking sheet.

14. Slam the tray, hard, 4-6 times on the counter. Then fist bump each side of the tray twice.

15. Let dry until they look dull but not overly dry. **Drying time varies on humidity. In a dry climate the macarons can dry in 15-20 minutes and in a humid climate it can take 35-40 minutes. But never dry them for more than an hour.

16. While the macarons are drying, preheat the oven to 325°F, 170°C.

17. Place on the middle rack of the oven.

18. Check in 14 minutes.

19. If their tops slide then bake for 2 -3 more minutes. They should release from the parchment or Silpat without sticking. Check one. If it sticks put them back in the oven for 1-2 more minutes.

19. Let them cool for a few minutes before removing from the Silpat or parchment paper.

• Vanilla Sponge Cake

This is an unusual sponge cake with the small amount of water added.
It has a delicious texture and flavor.

EQUIPMENT:
Stand mixer fitted with whisk attachment
Quarter sheet pan or 9 x 13" pan
Parchment paper
Spatula
2 Large bowls

INGREDIENTS:

177g	Cake Flour
1½ tsp	Baking Soda
¼ tsp	Salt
6	Eggs, separated
⅛ tsp	Cream of Tartar
283g	Sugar, divided
2 tsp	Vanilla Extract
71g	Water

1. Preheat oven to 350 degrees

2. Lightly spray the sides and bottom of the quarter sheet pan or 9 x 13" pan.

3. Line the bottom with a piece of parchment paper. Lightly spray the paper.

4. Sift together the cake flour, baking powder and salt 3 times.

5. In a stand mixer fitted with the whisk attachment whip the egg yolks, vanilla and first sugar until the mixture is thick and pale in color. It should be thick enough to hold a three second ribbon. (Test for this by detaching the whisk and waving it on top of the mixture, the batter that falls off the whisk should hold its shape on the surface for 3 seconds.)

6. Move the egg yolk mixture to a large bowl and wash the bowl and whisk.

7. Whip the egg whites and cream of tartar on medium speed until they are frothy and no longer liquid.

8. With the mixer running, "rain" in the sugar and whip on medium high speed until it looks shiny and soft (marshmallow fluff stage).

9. Turn the mixer to high and as the mixture begins to dull slightly, check for peak. The angle of the peak should be at 11:00, medium peak.

10. Gently fold 1/3rd of the egg whites into the egg yolks to lighten the mixture.

11. Add remaining egg whites. Add the flour in three increments, alternately with the water mixture. Do not overmix.

12. Pour the batter into the prepared pan. Bake for 20 minutes. Start checking. The cake is done when a skewer inserted into the center comes out clean and the sponge springs back lightly when touched.

Pastry Cream

Pastry cream will keep 3 days in the refrigerator.

EQUIPMENT:
Medium saucepan
Whisk
Spatula
Strainer
2 Medium bowls
Ice bath or plastic lined baking sheet,
for cooling pastry cream

INGREDIENTS:
342g Milk, divided
 86g Sugar, divided
 2 tsp Amoretti® Vanilla Bean Paste
2tbsp Cornstarch
   2 Egg Yolks
 14g Butter

1. In the saucepan, combine 285g milk, 43g sugar and vanilla bean paste. Bring to a simmer over medium heat.

2. Meanwhile, stir together cornstarch and 43g sugar. Whisk in 57g milk and egg yolks.

3. Temper the egg yolk mixture by pouring in half of the hot milk, whisking constantly. Add warmed egg yolk mixture to saucepan.

4. Whisk gently over medium heat until the mixture thickens. Whisk until smooth.

5. Remove pan from heat and whisk in the butter.

6. Cool over an ice bath with plastic wrap on the surface or pour into plastic lined pan, cover and chill until ready to use.

Ganache

EQUIPMENT:
Medium saucepan
Heatproof bowl
Spatula

INGREDIENTS:
113g Semi-sweet Chocolate
113g Heavy Cream

1. Place the chocolate in a heatproof bowl.

2. In a saucepan over medium heat, bring the cream to a simmer.

3. Pour the hot cream over the chocolate.

4. Let sit for 2-3 minutes then stir until smooth. It should be glossy and rich.

BOSTON CREAM PIE HISTORY

Boston Cream Pie was created in 1856 by a chef at the Parker House Hotel in Boston.

His name was M. Sanzian and he was French. He was inspired to create a dessert that would rival "Washington Pie," a popular dessert at that time.

Chef Sanzian layered vanilla sponge with pastry cream and topped it all off with chocolate "fondant".

The vanilla sponge was baked in a pie plate and the chocolate "fondant" was basically chocolate ganache.

The dessert was an instant hit and it's still on the menu at the Parker House today. Boston Cream Pie is the state dessert of Massachusetts. It also has its own day, that's pretty impressive.

October 23rd is Boston Cream Pie Day. Please don't wait until October 23rd to make our macaron variation.

Boston Creme Pie Macaron Cake *Assembly*

EQUIPMENT:
8" cardboard cake round
Spoon
Pastry brush
Piping bag
Medium plain tip (805 or 806)

1. If sponge is thick, trim top with a serrated knife.

2. Starting ½" from the edge, carefully hollow out the top ¼" of the sponge (see photo).

3. Place one macaron disk on the cardboard cake round and carefully slide the hollowed sponge on top of the macaron disk.

4. With the pastry brush, soak the sponge with vanilla simple syrup.

5. Fill piping bag, fitted with the plain tip, with pastry cream.

6. Pipe a layer of pastry cream on the sponge, starting in the center and finishing with a layer over the outer rim of the cake.

7. Top with remaining macaron disk.

8. Drizzle ganache on top.

Tres Leches Macaron Cake

COMPONENTS:

Coconut Macaron Disks
Tres Leches Sponge cut into 6" circles
Tres Leches Simple Syrup
Tres Leches Pastry Cream
Mango Gelée
1 ripe mango, cut into small dice

EQUIPMENT:

1. Stand or handheld mixer
2. Food processor
3. Instant read thermometer
4. Piping bag
5. Parchment paper or Silpats
6. 1 Half baking sheet
7. Flat rubber spatula
8. Large bowl
9. #12 Wilton tip or Ateco #803 or any plain round tip with a 3/8" diameter opening

INGREDIENTS:

100g	Powdered Sugar
75g	Almond Meal
25g	Unsweetened finely shredded (dessicated) Coconut
75g	Egg Whites
65g	Granulated Sugar
½ tsp	Vanilla Extract
drop	Orange Gel Color
drop	Amoretti® Coconut or Coconut Cream Extract

• Coconut Macaron Disks

Yield: Two 6" macaron shells. Serves 5-6.

Preheat oven to 325°F or 160°C (conventional), 300°F or 150°C (convection).

1. Line the bottom of a half sheet tray with a piece of parchment paper. Draw two 6" circles on the paper and turn it over so that the ink or pencil does not bleed onto the macaron. A silpat can be used on top of the template.

2. Layer the powdered sugar, almond meal and coconut in a food processor or mini-prep fitted with a metal blade.

3. Pulse the powdered sugar, almond meal and coconut in a food processor until the mixture looks like fine meal – about 15 seconds or 8 pulses. Remove the dry mixture from the food processor and transfer to a bowl.

4. Place the egg whites, sugar and a pinch of cream of tartar into the bowl of a stand mixer, whisk to combine. Make sure that the bowl and the whisk are impeccably clean.

5. Heat the egg whites and sugar to 120°F (49°C), whisk slowly as the mixture is heating. Use an instant read or candy thermometer – if you don't have a thermometer the mixture should feel very warm to the touch.

7. Carefully attach the hot mixer bowl to the mixer. Starting on medium speed, whip the egg whites until it looks like light foam. The egg whites should not appear liquid. The foam will be light and should not have any structure.

8. Continue to whip the meringue until it is soft and shiny. It should look like marshmallow fluff.

9. Add the color and extracts. Staying at medium high speed, whip the egg whites until they begins to dull and the lines of the whisk are visible on the surface of the meringue.

10. Now check for peak. The peak should be firm with the angle supporting the peak at 11:30. Transfer to a medium sized bowl.

11. Fold in the almond meal and powdered sugar in three increments.

12. Paint the mixture halfway up the side of the bowl, using the flat side of your spatula. Then scrape the mixture down to the center of the bowl.

13. Repeat 2-3 times then check to see if the mixture slides slowly down the side of the bowl.

14. Pipe on parchment or Silpat-lined baking sheets. Sprinkle a little coconut on top. Slam the tray, hard, 4-6 times on the counter. Then fist bump each side of the tray twice.

15. Let dry until they look dull but not overly dry. **Drying time varies on humidity. In a dry climate the macarons can dry in 15-20 minutes and in a humid climate it can take 35-40. But I never let them dry for over an hour.

16. While the macarons are drying, preheat the oven to 325°F, 160-170°C.

17. Place on the middle rack of the oven.

18. Check in 14 minutes.

19. If their tops slide, then bake for 2 -3 more minutes. They should release from the parchment or Silpat without sticking. Check one. If it sticks, put them back in the oven for 1-2 more minutes.

20. Let them cool for 10 minutes before removing from the Silpat or parchment paper.

• Tres Leches Sponge

EQUIPMENT:
Stand mixer fitted with whisk attachment
Quarter sheet pan or 9 x 13" pan
Parchment paper
Spatula
2 Large bowls

INGREDIENTS:

177g	Cake Flour
1½ tsp	Baking Soda
¼ tsp	Salt
6	Eggs, separated
⅛ tsp	Cream of Tartar
283g	Sugar, divided
2 tsp	Amoretti® Tres Leches or Vanilla Extract
71g	Water

1. Preheat the oven to 350°F.

2. Grease the pan and line the bottom with a piece of parchment paper.

3. In a large bowl, sift together flour, baking soda, and salt three times.

4. In a stand mixer fitted with the whisk attachment whip the egg yolks, extract and 198g sugar until the mixture is thick and pale in color. It should be thick enough to hold a three second ribbon. (Test for this by detaching the whisk and waving it on top of the mixture, the batter that falls off the whisk should hold its shape on the surface for 3 seconds.)

5. Move the egg yolk mixture to a large bowl and wash the bowl and whisk thoroughly.

6. In the mixer, whip the egg whites with the cream of tartar on medium speed until they look frothy and no egg white liquid remains.

7. With the mixer running, add the sugar slowly. Once the sugar is added turn the mixer on to medium high speed.

8. Continue to whip until the meringue is soft and shiny. At this stage it resembles "marshmallow fluff" and does not form a peak.

9. Turn the mixer to high speed, whip the egg whites until the mixture begins to look dull and the lines of the whisk are visible on the surface of the meringue. Now check for peak. The angle supporting the peak should be at 11:00, medium peak.

10. Gently fold ⅓rd of the egg whites into the egg yolks to lighten the mixture.

11. Fold in remaining egg whites.

12. Add the flour in three increments, alternating with the water. Do not overmix.

13. Pour the batter into the prepared pan. Bake for 20 minutes. The cake is done when a skewer inserted into the center comes out clean and the sponge springs back lightly when touched.

• Tres Leches Pastry Cream

EQUIPMENT:
Medium saucepan
Whisk
Spatula
Strainer
2 Medium bowls
Ice bath or plastic lined baking sheet,
for cooling pastry cream

INGREDIENTS:
170g Condensed Milk
171g Milk, divided
   1 Lime, zest only
1tbsp Cornstarch
   2 Egg Yolks
1 tsp Amoretti® Tres Leches Extract
        (rum, vanilla extract or rum
        extract may be used)

1. In the saucepan, combine condensed milk, 114g milk and lime zest. Bring mixture to a boil over medium heat, remove from heat and set aside for 1 hour. Strain out lime zest.

2. Return the lime infused milk to the saucepan and bring to a simmer.

3. Meanwhile, stir together cornstarch, 57g milk and egg yolks.

3. Temper the egg yolk mixture by pouring in half of the hot milk, whisking constantly. Add warmed egg yolk mixture to saucepan.

4. Whisk gently over medium heat until the mixture thickens. Whisk until smooth.

5. Remove pan from heat and whisk in the extract.

6. Cool over an ice bath with plastic wrap on the surface or pour into plastic lined pan, cover and chill until ready to use.

Pastry cream will keep 3 days in the refrigerator.

• Tres Leches Simple Syrup

EQUIPMENT:
Small saucepan
Whisk or spoon
Pastry brush

INGREDIENTS:
133g Water
133g Granulated Sugar
 2 tsp Amoretti® Tres Leches Extract

1. Bring water and sugar to a boil, stirring to dissolve sugar.

2. Once the sugar has dissolved and the syrup looks clear, remove pan from heat. Set aside to cool.

3. Add extract when syrup has cooled.

Refrigerated, syrup will keep 6 months.

● Mango Gelée

EQUIPMENT:
Small saucepan
Whisk
6" cake pan, lined with plastic wrap

INGREDIENTS:
2g Gelatin (1 sheet or ½ teaspoon powdered)
57g Sugar
57g Water
57g Mango Purée or Juice
2 tsp Lime Juice
1g Agar

1. Bloom the sheet gelatin by submerging it in very cold water for ten minutes until it softens. If using powdered gelatin, bloom it by sprinkling it over 2½ teaspoons of cold water – let it sit for 10 minutes.

2. Combine sugar, water, mango purée or juice, lime juice and agar in a saucepan.

3. Over medium heat, bring the mixture to a low boil and whisk to dissolve sugar. Let boil for 1 minute.

4. Remove from heat. Add gelatin.

5. Pour onto prepared pan and refrigerate until set, about 1 hour.

Tres Leches Macaron Cake *Assembly*

EQUIPMENT:
8" cardboard cake round
Spoon
Pastry brush
Piping bag
Medium plain tip (805 or 806)

1. If sponge is thick, trim top with a serrated knife.

2. Starting ½" from the edge, carefully hollow out the top ¼" of the sponge (see photo).

3. Place one macaron disk on the cardboard cake round and carefully slide the hollowed sponge on top of the macaron disk.

4. With the pastry brush, soak the sponge with tres leches simple syrup.

5. Fill piping bag, fitted with the plain tip, with tres leches pastry cream.

6. Pipe a layer of pastry cream on the sponge, starting in the center and finishing with a layer over the outer rim of the cake.

7. Sprinkle diced mango over pastry cream.

8. Place mango gelée over diced mango.

9. Top with remaining macaron disk.

S'mores Macaron Cake

COMPONENTS *(PER EACH S'MORE)***:**
Graham Cracker Macarons
Chocolate Ganache
Soft Marshmallow "Fluff"

EQUIPMENT:
1. Stand or handheld mixer
2. Food processor
3. Instant read thermometer
4. Piping bag
5. Parchment paper or Silpats
6. 1 Half baking sheet
7. Flat rubber spatula
8. Large bowl
9. #12 Wilton tip or Ateco #803 or any plain round tip with a 3/8" diameter opening

INGREDIENTS:
100g	Powdered Sugar
70g	Almond Meal
30g	Graham Cracker Crumbs, plus additional for sprinkling
75g	Egg Whites
65g	Granulated Sugar
½ tsp	Amoretti® S'mores Extract or Vanilla Extract

• Graham Cracker Macarons

Yield: Six 3 x 3" macaron shells. Serves 3-6.

Preheat oven to 325°F or 160°C (conventional), 300°F or 150°C (convection).

1. Line the bottom of a half sheet tray with a piece of parchment paper. Draw six 3x3" squares on the paper and turn it over so that the ink or pencil does not bleed onto the macaron. A silpat can be used on top of the template.

2. Layer the powdered sugar, almond meal and graham cracker crumbs in a food processor or mini-prep fitted with a metal blade.

3. Pulse the powdered sugar, almond meal and graham cracker crumbs in a food processor until the mixture looks like fine meal – about 15 seconds or 8 pulses. Remove the dry mixture from the food processor and transfer to a bowl.

4. Place the egg whites, sugar and a pinch of cream of tartar into the bowl of a stand mixer, whisk to combine. Make sure that the bowl and the whisk are impeccably clean.

5. Heat the egg whites and sugar to 120°F (49°C), whisk slowly as the mixture is heating. Use an instant read or candy thermometer – if you don't have a thermometer the mixture should feel very warm to the touch.

7. Carefully attach the hot mixer bowl to the mixer. Starting on medium speed, whip the egg whites until it looks like light foam. The egg whites should not appear liquid. The foam will be light and should not have any structure.

8. Continue to whip the meringue until it is soft and shiny. It should look like marshmallow fluff.

9. Add a few drops of extract. Staying at medium high speed, whip the egg whites until they begins to dull and the lines of the whisk are visible on the surface of the meringue.

10. Now check for peak. The peak should be firm with the angle supporting the peak at 11:30. Transfer to a medium sized bowl.

11. Fold in the almond meal and powdered sugar mixture in three increments.

12. Paint the mixture halfway up the side of the bowl, using the flat side of your spatula. Then scrape the mixture down to the center of the bowl.

13. Repeat 2-3 times then check to see if the mixture slides slowly down the side of the bowl.

14. Pipe on parchment or Silpat-lined baking sheets. Sprinkle graham cracker crumbs on top. Slam the tray, hard, 4-6 times on the counter. Fist bump each side of the tray twice.

15. Let dry until they look dull but not overly dry. **Drying time varies on humidity. In a dry climate the macarons can dry in 15-20 minutes and in a humid climate it can take 35-40. But I never let them dry for over an hour.

16. While the macarons are drying, preheat the oven to 325°F, 160-170°C.

16. Place on the middle rack of the oven. Check after 14 minutes.

19. If their tops slide, then bake for 2 -3 more minutes. They should release from the parchment or Silpat without sticking. Check one. If it sticks, put them back in the oven for 1-2 more minutes.

20. Let them cool for 10 minutes before removing from the Silpat or parchment paper.

• Chocolate Ganache

EQUIPMENT:
Medium saucepan
Heatproof bowl
Spatula

INGREDIENTS:
113g Semi-sweet Chocolate
113g Heavy Cream

1. Place the chocolate in a heatproof bowl.

2. In a saucepan over medium heat, bring the cream to a simmer.

3. Pour the hot cream over the chocolate.

4. Let sit for 2-3 minutes then stir until smooth. Cover and refrigerate until set.

• Soft Marshmallow "Fluff"

EQUIPMENT:
Medium saucepan
Stand mixer fitted with the whisk attachment
Candy thermometer

INGREDIENTS:
2½ tsp Very Cold Water
1½ tsp Powdered Gelatin**
4oz Water, divided
6oz Sugar
5oz Corn Syrup
1 tsp Vanilla Extract

1. In the mixer bowl, sprinkle gelatin over 2½ tsp water and let sit 5 minutes to dissolve.

2. Add an additional 2oz water to gelatin and turn mixer to low speed.

3. Meanwhile, add the last 2oz water, sugar and corn syrup to the saucepan. Bring to a boil and cook, without stirring, to 240°F (soft ball stage).

3. Lock the lip of the pot to the edge of the mixer bowl and pour the hot sugar over the gelatin.

4. Once all the sugar is in, turn the mixer to high and whisk 5-7 minutes. The mixture will become very thick and fluffy.

5. Add vanilla and mix to combine.

**3 sheets of gelatin bloomed in cold water can be used in place of powdered gelatin. Omit the 2½ tsp of water.

S'mores Macaron Cake *Assembly*

EQUIPMENT:
Crème brûlée torch or broiler
Offset spatula
Piping bag
Medium plain tip (805 or 806)

1. On the flat side of one macaron, spread a generous layer of ganache.

2. Pipe a layer of marshmallow fluff over ganache.

3. Place macaron on a heatproof surface, like a metal baking sheet.

3. Carefully toast the top of the marshmallow fluff with the torch. Alternately, toast under a broiler. Do not walk away! Watch closely until desired level of toastiness has been achieved.

4. Top with remaining macaron.

 NOTES

Macaron Towers & Embellishing

Building a macaron tower is a great way to expand your macaron skill set.

Building a Macaron Tower

These beautiful towers are not difficult to make, they just take some time and a little patience. The results are worth it. What better way to showcase your beautiful work? The size of the tower is up to you.

EQUIPMENT:
Styrofoam cone
Pastry brush
Decorative base

COMPONENTS:
Finished macarons, assorted sizes,
   filled with buttercream or
   ganache (avoid soft fillings)
8oz Royal icing,
   colored to match macarons
Decorative elements
   (candy, sugar flowers, etc.)

Macaron Tower *Assembly*

1. Paint the cone with royal icing – it may take two coats to cover the cone.

2. Let dry half-way.

3. Attach the macarons to the cone with tooth picks or royal icing. I prefer gluing the macarons down with royal icing.

4. Use a spiral pattern when attaching the macarons.

5. Let sit until dry.

Violet Spun Sugar

Spun sugar does not last long unfortunately, this part of the showpiece cannot be made in advance. Be very careful when working with hot sugar.

EQUIPMENT:
Saucepan with tall sides
Candy thermometer
Dry towel
2 Rolling pins or dowels, greased
Newspaper or parchment to
    protect the floor
Whisk with top removed
    (also called a truncated whisk
    or sugar spinner).

INGREDIENTS:
 50g Water
500g Isomalt
Purple Color, gel or water soluble
    powder

1. Place the water in the saucepan and bring to a boil. Add a small amount of isomalt stirring occasionally until the isomalt dissolves. Continue adding isomalt until it is all melted.

2. Once the isomalt is dissolved and boiling start checking temperatures.

3. At 300°F add color.

4. At 340°F remove from heat. Place the pot on a dry towel that has been placed on a heat proof surface.

5. Let the isomalt stand undisturbed for 10 minutes.

6. Line up the two greased dowels so they hang over the floor. Place newspaper or parchment on the floor underneath the dowels.

7. After 10 minutes test the isomalt by dipping a spoon in the pan and lifting it out, the syrup flowing back to the pan should look like a thread.

8. Once the isomalt is the correct consistency, dip the end of the whisk in the isomalt and then swing or flick the threads over the oiled dowels.

9. Continue until you have enough.

Unfortunately, cleaning up after making spun sugar is a bit of a mess. To make it easier, fill the pot up more than halfway with water and boil out the sugar – the whisk can go in the pot too.

Royal Icing

EQUIPMENT:
Stand or handheld mixer fitted
   with paddle attachment
Airtight container
Damp paper towel

INGREDIENTS:
454g Powdered Sugar
28g Meringue Powder
5-6 tbsp Water

1. Combine the powdered sugar and meringue powder in the mixer.

2. Mix one minute on low speed until combined.

3. Add the water, mix on medium low until the ingredients are combined.

4. Increase speed to medium high and mix for 5-6 minutes. The icing should be thick and form thick peaks.

5. Store in an airtight container with a damp paper towel on the surface of the royal icing. Do not refrigerate.

Using meringue powder eliminates any risk of salmonella and is safer to use than raw egg whites. It is available online, at craft stores and cake decorating shops.

Decorating Macarons

Now that the techniques are mastered - here's how to decorate your macarons.

Macarons can be embellished with **luster dust, petal dust, powdered food color** (see note below), **food grade markers** and **edible glitters**.

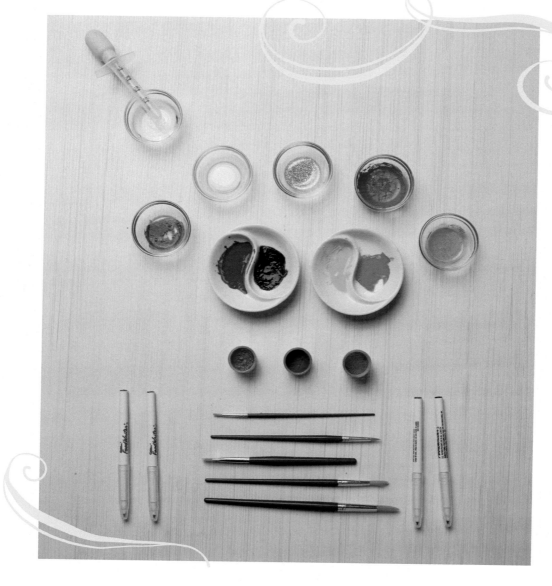

Liquid color can bleed into the macaron with the exception of white liquid color. Amoretti's "Snow White" food color works great, it is opaque and does not need to be diluted with water. Its less romantic name is Titanium Dioxide. It can also be used to lighten other colors.

Luster Dust & Petal Dust

EQUIPMENT:
Luster dust or petal dust
Food grade dry brush

TECHNIQUE:
This is the easiest embellishment of all.
Using a dry brush, apply luster dust to the
surface of the macarons with light strokes.

Striping - *brush with luster dust and vodka for a shimmery striped effect*

EQUIPMENT:
Luster dust or petal dust
Vodka
Small container to mix colors
Eyedropper (optional)
Food grade brushes

TECHNIQUE:
Mix vodka into the powders a little at a time,
an eye dropper works best.
Brush stripes of color on the macarons.
Let each color dry before adding the next color.

Both Wilton and Ateco make food grade artist's brushes -
they are inexpensive and the bristles don't fall out.

Painting

EQUIPMENT:

Luster dust, petal dust, or powdered food color
Vodka
Small container to mix colors
Eyedropper (optional)
Food grade brushes
Food grade markers

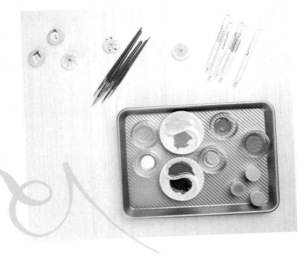

TECHNIQUE:

When painting macarons, you are limited
only by your imagination. Set up a palate
of your favorite colors and have fun.
Food grade markers are great for layering
in colors or writing messages.
**Colors dry out quickly, keep the vodka handy.*

118

CALLA LILLY TECHNIQUE:

Using white food color, paint a teardrop shape. Add yellow and orange to the center of the white teardrop, for depth (see photo for reference). Finish with leaves at the base using green color or food grade marker.

SUNFLOWER TECHNIQUE:

Create the base flower with yellow color.
Highlight with gold and/or orange color, radiating from the center.
Add sunflower "seeds" with a brown food grade marker.
Finish with leaves, easiest with a green food grade marker.

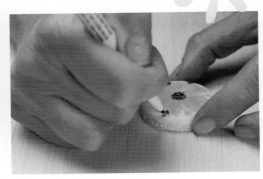

NOTES

Troubleshooting

Identifying what can go wrong and how to fix it.

In the years that I have been teaching and baking macarons, I have identified 7 things that can go wrong with macarons during mixing, drying and baking.

1. Rough, bumpy-looking shells and dry, cracked feet

Why this happens:

The meringue was over-whipped.
Symptoms include:

- The batter is very thick.
- Peaks on the surface of the shell.
- The shell will not be smooth and have small bumps on it.
- The feet will be high and cracked, especially where the shell meets the top of the foot.

OVERDEVELOPED MERINGUE HAS NO PEAK AND ANGLE IS STRAIGHT UP (NO CURVE).

OVER-MIXED MACARONS, AFTER BAKING

2. Cracked and misshapen shells

Why this happens:

- Not enough air was knocked out of the batter during the macaronnage process.
- The oven was too hot and the steam in the macaron expanded too quickly.
- The macarons did not dry long enough and there was not enough surface tension to contain the expanding macaron.

UNDER DRIED MACARONS AFTER BAKING

DRYING YOUR MACARONS

- *The reason for drying is to create surface tension on the surface of the shell.*
- *As the moisture in the macaron batter expands, steam is created and lifts the shell off the foot.*
- *The surface tension caused by letting the shell dry out slightly helps to contain the expansion of steam, so that the macaron shell stays intact and does not crack.*
- *When the macarons have not dried long enough the foot does not form properly. It pushes out rather then up and looks like a frill rather than a foot.*

OVER-MIXED (MACRONNAGED) BATTER
BEFORE AND AFTER BAKING

3. Thin and runny batter, "frill" instead of foot (pied)

Why this happens:

Over macaronnage – over mixing the batter after the dry ingredients are incorporated. Symptoms include:

- The batter is runny and difficult to pipe.
- The shell spreads and the feet (if they form) are shallow.
- There are spots on the surface of the shell.
- The foot does not lift properly, forming a frill rather than a foot.

PERFECTING YOUR MACARONNAGE

- *It is important to stop folding <u>as soon as</u> all the dry ingredients are incorporated.*
- *The goal of macronnage is to knock out excess air. The easiest way to achieve this (I feel) is to paint the batter halfway up the side of the bowl several times until it slides at the perfect speed down the side of the bowl.*
- *How fast it is moving down the side of the bowl is subjective. In my classes, it is usually the second batch where students get that "Ah-ha! I see it!" moment. "Not too fast, not too slow."*

4. Shells stick to parchment/Silpat

Why this happens:

Macarons were under-baked. Try this:

- Typically, small macarons (about 1½" in diameter) take about 11 minutes to bake at 325°F. Each oven is different; it can take a little trial and error to find that magic time for perfectly baked macarons.
- If this is realized early and the macarons are still warm and the baking tray hot, they can go back into the oven for 2-3 minutes to set. If the tray has cooled down, sadly, there is no going back. It would take too long for the macaron to heat up and set properly.

UNDER-BAKED MACARONS

5. Dry, crunchy shells

Why this happens:

Macarons were over-baked. It could be they were baked too long or the oven was too hot. Symptoms include:

- They lose vibrancy as the color bakes out. Royal blue turns khaki, purples turn gray, yellow turns tan.
- The surface of the macarons will look toasted.
- Silver lining - if they aren't too toasty, the over-baked shells can be ground up and used to decorate cakes or sprinkled on cupcakes.

OVER-BAKED MACARONS ARE DRY & CRUNCHY

6. Thin, hollow and translucent shells

Why this happens:

- Too much extract or color added to the shell. Alcohol from an extract and extra water from a food color thin out the shell as it bakes.
- Alcohol thins the egg white protein and makes a thin, sometimes splotchy shell.

THIN, SPLOTCHY SHELLS

7. Large air pocket under shell surface

Why this happens:

- Not enough air was knocked out of the batter. This usually happens in the "painting and scraping" stage (macronnage), right after the dry ingredients are incorporated.
- It was rapped too gently or not at all.
- As the macaron bakes, the expanding steam lifts not only the shell but the extra air.

HOLLOW MACARONS

 NOTES

Resources

Here is a list of sources for ingredients and equipment.

- Amoretti.com
- Amazon.com
- Kingarthurflour.com
- Surlatable.com
- Williams-sonoma.com
- Fantes.com
- Chefrubber.com
- Wilton.com

Index